Sunset Cook Book of Desserts

A reissue of an award-winning Sunset book for which we have had a great many requests. Our new cover reflects the interest in light desserts, a number of which have been added to the book.

Sunset Cook Book of

Desserts

BY THE EDITORS OF SUNSET BOOKS
AND SUNSET MAGAZINE

Lane Publishing Co.• Menlo Park, California

Cover: Raspberry Frozen Fruit Yogurt (see page 56) and rolled-up *Cialde* (see page 84). Photographed by Tom Wyatt. Photograph on page 2 (Mocha-Pecan Flan—see page 45) and page 24 by Glenn Christiansen. All other photographs by Darrow M. Watt. Illustrations by Frank L. Lanza.

Editor, Sunset Books: David E. Clark
Eighth Printing April 1978
Copyright © 1968, 1963, Lane Publishing Co., Menlo Park, CA 94025.
Second Edition. World rights reserved.

Contents

Cakes

Dessert spectaculars have the spotlight here. Guests can't fail to appreciate the unreservedly elegant layer cakes, tube cakes, yeast cakes, cheesecakes, tortes, fruit cakes, and splendid meringue cakes. These dazzlers can be featured as centerpieces as well as desserts; each is certain to bring lavish compliments to the cook.

In addition to these glamorous creations (even the most involved of them is described in easy-to-accomplish steps), there are also simpler, quick-to-make cakes that can be served without embellishment for a family meal or to accompany mid-day coffee. Frosting and a little decoration will convert many of them into party desserts, if desired.

Sour Cream Cake

There's no describing this sour cream cake. The nuance of almonds and the tang of lemon are an unusually good combination.

1 cup (½ lb.) butter or margarine, at
room temperature
3¼ cups sugar
1 tablespoon lemon or orange extract
1 teaspoon almond extract
6 eggs
¼ teaspoon soda
3 cups all-purpose flour, unsifted
1 cup sour cream
2 tablespoons lemon or orange juice

In a large bowl, beat together butter, 3 cups of the sugar, lemon extract, and almond extract. Add eggs, one at a time, beating after each addition. Stir soda into flour; add flour mixture and sour cream alternately to the creamed mixture, mixing just until blended.

Sugar-dusted Buttermilk-Orange
Poundcake (recipe, page 9) is
flavored with orange, topped with
juicy fresh fruits.

Spoon batter into a well-greased 10-inch tube pan. Bake in a 325° oven for about 1½ hours or until a wooden pick inserted in center comes out clean. Cool cake in pan for about 15 minutes, then turn out.

Mix remaining ¼ cup sugar and lemon juice; drizzle over cake. Cool. Makes 10 to 12 servings.

Marmalade Meringue Torte

This two-layer cake becomes a four-layer torte with orange marmalade between the layers and a light meringue frosting.

1 package (about 1 lb. 3 oz.) yellow,
white, or lemon-flavored cake mix
1½ cups orange marmalade
4 egg whites
⅛ teaspoon salt
¾ cup brown sugar

Make a 2-layer cake from cake mix as directed; bake and cool. Split both layers to make 4 layers. Spread ½ cup marmalade on each of 3 layers; stack, put plain layer on top, and set aside.

Beat egg whites with salt until foamy. Gradually add brown sugar; beat until stiff. Frost sides and top of cake with this meringue. Bake in a hot oven (400°) for 5 minutes or until lightly browned. Makes 8 servings.

Old-fashioned Poundcake

This rich, extra-moist cake can be served plain, with powdered sugar on top, or covered with fresh sliced fruit.

*2 cups each butter or margarine, at
   room temperature, and sugar
9 eggs, separated
1½ teaspoons vanilla
3 tablespoons brandy or ¼ teaspoon
   brandy extract
4 cups sifted cake flour or 3½ cups
   sifted all-purpose flour
1 teaspoon ground mace or nutmeg
½ teaspoon each cream of tartar
   and salt*

Beat butter and 1½ cups of the sugar together until very creamy and fluffy (about 5 minutes on medium speed of an electric mixer). Add egg yolks, one at a time, beating after each addition; beat in vanilla and brandy until blended.

Sift flour again with mace, cream of tartar, and salt; gradually add to creamy mixture, beating until thoroughly blended.

In a large bowl, beat egg whites until frothy. Begin adding remaining ½ cup sugar, 2 tablespoons at a time, beating after each addition; continue beating until stiff, glossy peaks form. Carefully fold about ¼ of the batter at a time into whites until blended.

Turn batter into a greased and floured 10-inch tube pan, a 12-cup fluted tube cake pan, or two 5 by 9-inch loaf pans. Bake in a 325° oven until a long wooden pick inserted in center comes out clean (about 1 hour for loaf pans or about 1 hour and 15 minutes for tube pans). Makes 25 servings.

Spiced Pumpkin Roll

To climax Thanksgiving or any autumn meal, offer a spongy pumpkin cake filled with ice cream.

*¾ cup all-purpose flour, unsifted
2 teaspoons ground cinnamon
1 teaspoon each baking powder and
   ground ginger
½ teaspoon each ground nutmeg and
   salt
3 eggs
1 cup granulated sugar
⅔ cup canned pumpkin
Powdered sugar
1 quart toasted almond or vanilla ice
   cream, slightly softened*

Mix flour, cinnamon, baking powder, ginger, nutmeg, and salt; set aside. In a large bowl, beat eggs at high speed for 5 minutes or until thick; gradually beat in granulated sugar. Using low speed, mix in pumpkin and flour mixture.

Line a 10 by 15-inch greased jelly roll pan with waxed paper; grease paper. Spread batter in pan. Bake in a 375° oven for 15 minutes, or until top springs back when touched. Immediately invert cake onto a towel sprinkled with powdered sugar.

Remove paper; roll cake and towel into a cylinder and cool completely. Unroll cake, spread with ice cream, and reroll. Wrap and freeze. Before serving, let stand at room temperature 10 to 15 minutes; dust with powdered sugar. Makes 8 to 10 servings.

Quick Carob Cake

This quick-to-make cake uses roasted carob powder (sold as a chocolate substitute in natural or health food stores).

*1½ cups all-purpose flour, unsifted
1 cup sugar
¼ cup roasted carob powder
1 teaspoon soda
½ teaspoon salt
⅓ cup salad oil
1 tablespoon vinegar
1 teaspoon vanilla
1 cup cold water*

Combine flour, sugar, carob powder, soda, and salt; sift into a bowl. Make a well in flour mixture and pour in salad oil, vinegar, vanilla, and cold water. Stir just until blended.

Spread batter into a greased 9-inch-square pan. Bake in a 350° oven for 25 minutes or until a wooden pick inserted in center comes out clean. Cool. Makes 8 servings.

Chocolate Almond Carrot Cake

Ground almonds and bread crumbs replace flour in this moist, crunchy carrot cake. Orange peel and chocolate flavor it.

1 cup whole almonds
2 ounces semisweet chocolate, cut
   in chunks
6 eggs, separated
1 cup sugar
1 tablespoon grated orange peel
¾ teaspoon ground cinnamon
¼ teaspoon salt
½ cup fine dry bread crumbs
1 cup grated carrots, lightly packed
Chocolate Frosting (recipe below)

Whirl almonds in a blender or food processor until finely ground. Generously butter inside of a 9-inch tube pan (with removable bottom); sprinkle with 2 tablespoons of the ground almonds. Set aside remaining ground almonds. Whirl chocolate until ground; also set aside.

In a large bowl, beat egg whites until foamy; then add ¼ cup of the sugar, a tablespoon at a time, beating until stiff, moist, glossy peaks form.

In a small bowl, beat egg yolks with remaining ¾ cup sugar, orange peel, cinnamon, and salt until thick. Stir in remaining almonds and bread crumbs. Press out excess liquid from carrots; then gently stir into egg yolk mixture. Pour half of the carrot mixture over egg whites and gently fold in; then fold in chocolate and remaining carrot mixture until blended. Spread batter into pan.

Bake in a 350° oven for about 45 minutes or until wooden pick inserted into center comes out clean. Cool thoroughly in pan. Remove cake and spread top with frosting. Makes 8 servings.

Chocolate Frosting

2 tablespoons butter or margarine
1 ounce semisweet chocolate
1 cup powdered sugar
2 tablespoons hot water
Almond slices (optional)

In a small pan, melt butter and chocolate over low heat. Stir in powdered sugar and hot water, beating with a spoon until smooth. Spread over top of cake; decorate with almond slices if desired.

Buttermilk-Orange Poundcake

Though not a true pound cake, this orange-flavored version resembles one in texture and richness.

½ cup butter or margarine
2½ cups sugar
4 eggs
3 cups all-purpose flour, unsifted
½ teaspoon soda
¾ cup buttermilk
¼ cup Cointreau or other orange-
   flavored liqueur
1 tablespoon grated orange peel
1 teaspoon vanilla
Sliced fruit (optional)

With an electric mixer, beat butter until creamy. Gradually beat in sugar until mixture is light and fluffy. Add eggs, one at a time, beating 2 minutes after each addition. Mix flour and soda together; set aside. Blend buttermilk, Cointreau, orange peel, and vanilla. Add flour mixture and buttermilk mixture alternately to creamed mixture, beginning and ending with dry ingredients. Beat well after each addition.

Pour batter into a greased and flour-dusted 10-inch tube pan or fancy tube mold that holds about 12 cups. Bake in a 350° oven for about 1 hour and 5 minutes or until a wooden pick inserted in center comes out clean. Cool cake in pan for 10 minutes, then turn out onto a rack to cool completely.

Dust with powdered sugar just before serving and top with fruit, if desired. Makes 10 to 12 servings.

Royal Pineapple Torte

4 eggs, separated
¾ cup plus 2 tablespoons sugar
1 cup cake flour (sift before measuring)
1 teaspoon baking powder
¼ teaspoon salt
1 cup canned crushed pineapple,
    well drained
1 cup chopped walnuts
Pineapple Butter Frosting (recipe
    follows)

Grease well two 8-inch layer pans; line with waxed paper, then grease the paper. Beat egg yolks until thick. Gradually add ½ the sugar, beating thoroughly. Beat egg whites until stiff; gradually add remaining sugar, beating until smooth and glossy. Carefully fold yolk mixture into beaten whites. Sift flour again with baking powder and salt; carefully fold into egg mixture, about 2 tablespoons at a time. Fold in pineapple and walnuts. Turn into greased pans. Bake in a moderate oven (350°) for 30 minutes or until cake shrinks from pan sides. Remove from pans; cool. Spread Pineapple Butter Frosting between layers, and over top and sides of torte. Makes 6 to 8 servings.

Pineapple Butter Frosting

¼ cup (⅛ lb.) butter
1¾ cups sifted powdered sugar
1 teaspoon vanilla
Dash salt
⅓ cup well-drained crushed pineapple

Cream butter. Gradually beat in sifted powdered sugar. Add vanilla, salt, and pineapple.

Sour Cream Banana Spice Cake

2 eggs, separated
½ cup (¼ pound) butter or margarine
1½ cups brown sugar, firmly packed
2 cups all-purpose flour (sift before
    measuring)
1 teaspoon each soda and cinnamon
½ teaspoon each salt and ground cloves
½ cup mashed ripe bananas
½ cup commercial sour cream
1 teaspoon vanilla
½ cup finely chopped nuts

Beat egg whites until stiff but not dry; set aside. Cream together butter and sugar; beat in egg yolks. Sift flour again with soda, cinnamon, salt, and ground cloves. Mix together bananas, sour cream, and vanilla. Add dry ingredients to creamed mixture alternately with banana mixture. Fold in egg whites. Pour into greased, 9-inch square cake pan. Sprinkle with nuts. Bake in a moderate oven (350°) for 45 minutes or until a wooden pick inserted in center comes out clean. Makes 9 servings.

Old-fashioned Devil's Food Cake

This is a rich chocolate cake that stays moist for several days when stored airtight.

2 squares (1 oz. each) unsweetened
    chocolate
½ cup butter or margarine
1 cup sugar
1 teaspoon vanilla
2 eggs
1½ cups cake flour (sift before measuring)
¾ teaspoon soda
1 teaspoon salt
¾ cup ice water
Chocolate Frosting (recipe follows)

Melt chocolate, then cool. Meanwhile, cream butter with sugar, beating until light and fluffy. Add vanilla, then eggs, one at a time, beating well after each addition. Blend in cooled, melted chocolate.

Sift flour again with soda and salt. Add flour to creamed mixture alternately with ice water; mix well.

Turn into a greased and floured 9-inch-square pan. Bake in a 350° oven for 30 to 35 minutes, or until cake pulls away from sides of pan. Cool and frost.

Chocolate Frosting

1 cup sugar
½ teaspoon salt
½ cup cream
1 square (1 oz.) chocolate, cut up
½ teaspoon vanilla
Small amount of cream (optional)
½ cup chopped walnuts (optional)

Blend together in a heavy saucepan the sugar, salt, ½ cup cream, and chocolate. Cover and boil over high heat for 3 minutes without stirring. Reduce heat, uncover, and continue cooking until frosting reaches the soft ball stage (238° on a candy thermometer). Wipe crystals from sides of pan but do not stir. Cool.

Beat frosting until creamy and a good spreading consistency. Add vanilla and, if frosting should become too thick, add a small amount of cream; beat until smooth. Spread on top of cake. Sprinkle with walnuts, if desired. Makes 6 servings.

Gingercake Shortcake

The creamy banana sauce is delicious in combination with this spicy gingerbread.

¼ cup (⅛ lb.) butter, at room
  temperature
¼ cup sugar
1 egg
½ cup light molasses
1¼ cups all-purpose flour (sift
  before measuring)
1 teaspoon each soda and salt
¼ teaspoon each ground nutmeg and
  ground ginger
½ cup hot water

Cream butter, sugar, and egg until light and fluffy. Beat in the molasses. Sift flour again with soda, salt, nutmeg, and ginger, and add to creamy mixture alternately with the water. Mix to a smooth batter. Turn into a greased and floured 8-inch square baking pan.

Bake in a hot oven (400°) for about 20 minutes. Cut into squares and serve hot with the Glazed Banana Sauce. Makes 9 servings.

Glazed Banana Sauce

¼ cup (⅛ lb.) butter or margarine
½ cup brown sugar, firmly packed
2 tablespoons orange juice
½ cup half-and-half (light cream) or
  whipping cream
4 bananas

Measure butter, sugar, and orange juice into a frying pan. Heat until the mixture is bubbly and well blended. Add cream and simmer about 4 or 5 minutes longer. Peel bananas and slice into bite-size pieces. Just before removing sauce from the heat, add the bananas. (Don't let the bananas cook long enough to become mushy.) Split the warm gingercake squares and spoon the warm sauce between the squares and over the top. Makes sauce for 6 servings.

Baba au Rhum

To one recipe of Savarin (see page 19), add ½ cup seedless currants and ½ cup golden raisins dusted with 1 tablespoon flour, just before turning batter into baking mold. Mix until fruits are evenly distributed.

Butter an 8-cup baba mold and turn mixture into it; or fill buttered individual baba molds (1 cup size) no more than half full. Let rise in a warm place until almost doubled (about 1 hour). Bake in a moderately hot oven (375°) for 35 to 40 minutes for the large baba, 15 to 20 minutes for small babas.

While baba is baking, make a rum-flavored syrup (see syrup recipe given with Savarin recipe, page 19). With a fork, prick surface of baba while still in mold. Turn out and prick top. Baste several times with syrup until cake is thoroughly soaked. Serve with additional rum syrup, and ice cream, if you wish. Makes 8 servings.

Chocolate Spice Chiffon Cake

The classic flavors of a European chocolate torte distinguish this chiffon cake. Spread chocolate frosting over the cake and decorate the top with whole filberts. Or you can serve it without frosting; top each slice with a mixture of chopped nuts and whipped cream. For the summer season, spoon plain whipped cream over the individual slices and surround each with fresh strawberries.

½ cup sweet ground chocolate
¾ cup boiling water
1½ cups all-purpose flour (sift
   before measuring)
1¾ cups sugar
4 teaspoons baking powder
¾ teaspoon salt
2 teaspoons ground allspice
1 teaspoon ground cinnamon
7 eggs, separated
½ cup salad oil
2 teaspoons grated orange peel
½ teaspoon cream of tartar
1 cup filberts or walnuts, finely chopped
Chocolate Frosting (see recipe on
   page 13)

Stir chocolate and boiling water until smooth; cool. Sift flour again into a bowl with 1½ cups of the sugar, baking powder, salt, allspice, and cinnamon. Make a well in the dry ingredients and add egg yolks, oil, orange peel, and cooled chocolate. Stir until smooth. Begin beating egg whites; when foamy, add cream of tartar and gradually beat in the remaining ¼ cup sugar until very stiff and satiny. Gently fold the chocolate mixture into the beaten whites. Sprinkle nuts on top; fold in (do not stir). Bake in a 10-inch ungreased tube pan in a moderate oven (350°) for 1 hour. Invert pan; cool. Frost with Chocolate Frosting, if desired. Makes 10 servings.

Rum Cake de Maison

Almost every cook likes to bring forth on occasion a dessert that can be described as a "creation." Rum Cake de Maison fits this description in all respects. It's a production, no denying, but one that can be accomplished leisurely in stages: Bake the orange and rum-flavored cake; make the whipped cream filling; mix the chocolate frosting; then assemble this dessert to chill *at least* 24 hours before serving.

2 cups cake flour (sift before measuring)
2 teaspoons baking powder
¼ teaspoon each salt and soda
½ cup (¼ pound) butter
1 cup sugar
2 eggs, separated
1 teaspoon grated orange peel
½ cup each orange juice and light rum
¼ teaspoon almond extract
½ teaspoon vanilla
Whipped Cream Filling (recipe follows)
Chocolate Frosting (recipe follows)
½ cup finely chopped walnuts

Sift flour again with baking powder, salt, and soda. Cream together butter and ¾ cup of the sugar until fluffy. Beat in egg yolks and orange peel. Blend orange juice with 3 tablespoons of the rum, almond extract, and vanilla; add alternately with flour to the creamed mixture. Whip egg whites until stiff; gradually beat in remaining ¼ cup sugar until whites hold stiff peaks. Fold into batter.

Butter two 8 or 9-inch round cake pans and line with waxed paper. Fill with equal portions of the batter. Bake in a moderate oven (350°) for 25 minutes or until cake begins to shrink from edges of pan. Cool layers 5 minutes in pan, then invert on wire racks, peel off paper, and let cool. Split each layer crosswise, making four thin layers.

To assemble cake, sprinkle each layer with remaining rum, and spread whipped cream filling between layers. Coat sides and top with chocolate frosting; pat walnuts on cake sides. Chill 24 hours before serving.

Whipped Cream Filling

2 teaspoons unflavored gelatin
2 tablespoons cold water
2 cups whipping cream
½ cup powdered sugar
⅓ cup light rum

Soften gelatin in cold water; dissolve over hot water. In a well chilled bowl, whip cream until it begins to thicken. Add powdered sugar and gradually blend in rum. Slowly pour in gelatin mixture, beating until just stiff enough to hold shape. Use immediately, or chill and blend again when ready to use.

Chocolate Frosting

*4 squares (4 ounces) melted
   unsweetened chocolate
1 cup sifted powdered sugar
2 tablespoons hot water
2 eggs
6 tablespoons butter, at room
   temperature*

Beat together melted chocolate and powdered sugar, gradually adding hot water. Beat in eggs, one at a time, and butter, mixing until smooth.

Prune Spice Cake

Here's a dark, moist, spice cake that's good with or without frosting.

*½ cup shortening
1 cup sugar
1 whole egg
2 egg yolks
1 cup pitted and chopped prunes (use
   moist-pack dried prunes or
   well-drained stewed prunes)
2 cups all-purpose flour (sift before
   measuring)
2 teaspoons baking powder
1 teaspoon each soda and ground
   cinnamon
½ teaspoon salt
About ½ teaspoon ground nutmeg
¼ teaspoon ground allspice
½ cup buttermilk
½ to 1 cup chopped nuts (optional)
Snow White Frosting (recipe follows)*

Cream the shortening and sugar together until fluffy. Add the whole egg and egg yolks and beat well. Blend in prunes. Sift flour into the creamed mixture with the baking powder, soda, cinnamon, salt, nutmeg, and allspice. Stir until blended. Mix in buttermilk until blended. Stir in the chopped nuts, if you use them.

Turn into two greased 8-inch layer cake pans and bake in a moderate oven (350°) for 35 to 40 minutes

or until the cake starts to pull away from the sides of the pan. Remove from the oven. Cool about 5 minutes, then turn out of pans and cool thoroughly. Frost between layers, on top, and sides with Snow White Frosting. Sprinkle top with nutmeg. Makes 8 servings.

Snow White Frosting

*2 egg whites
⅔ cup sugar
½ cup light corn syrup
2 tablespoons water*

Combine all the ingredients in the top of a double boiler and beat for 1 minute. Place over boiling water and beat with an electric mixer for 3 minutes or a rotary beater for 7 minutes, or until stiff peaks form. Scrape sides and bottom of pan occasionally. Remove from heat and continue beating until mixture cools.

Strawberry Torte

*1 package (2 layer size) lemon
   cake mix
4 cups whole, fully ripe strawberries
1 egg white
¾ cup sugar
⅛ teaspoon salt
⅛ teaspoon cream of tartar*

Bake cake in two 9-inch layer pans, following package directions. Cool before frosting. Pick out 8 to 10 large berries, with stems if possible; halve remaining.

To make the frosting, in top of a double boiler combine egg white, sugar, salt, cream of tartar, and ¾ cup halved strawberries. Beat with an electric mixer until fluffy. Set over slowly simmering water (water shouldn't touch upper pan) and continue beating with mixer for 7 minutes. Frosting will stand by itself in soft peaks.

Remove from heat and set in pan of cold water; beat with mixer about 2 minutes, or until frosting is cooled almost to room temperature. Then spread half the frosting over the top of each cake layer. (Refrigerate the frosted layers until you're ready to assemble the torte — up to 3 or 4 hours, if you wish.)

To assemble the cake, put a frosted layer on the serving plate. Arrange remaining 2 cups halved berries, cut side down, over this layer. Carefully put second cake layer on top of the first; arrange the whole strawberries on top. Let stand in a cool place until serving time. Makes 8 to 10 servings.

Three-Way Cheesecake

This luxuriantly rich cake lends itself to an intriguing group of variations.

Crumb lining

1½ cups zwieback crumbs
3 tablespoons sugar
⅓ cup melted butter

Blend together the crumbs, sugar, and butter, and press over bottom and sides of an 8 or 9-inch spring-form pan.

Basic cheesecake

3 large packages (8 oz.) cream cheese,
  at room temperature
1 tablespoon vanilla
½ teaspoon salt
4 large eggs
1 cup sugar

Blend softened cream cheese with vanilla and salt. In a large bowl, beat eggs very well, until thick. Beat in sugar gradually until mixture is lemon colored. Continue beating while you add cream cheese mixture in small portions, mixing each time until smooth. Turn into the crumb-lined pan. Bake in a moderate oven (350°) until cake jiggles slightly in center when gently shaken, about 25 to 30 minutes. Cool. Remove sides from pan and spread cake with lemon topping or sour cream topping. Makes 12 servings.

Lemon Topping

⅔ cup sugar
3 tablespoons cornstarch
¼ teaspoon salt
¾ cup boiling water
1 egg, beaten
1 tablespoon butter
3 tablespoons lemon juice
½ teaspoon each grated lemon peel
  and vanilla

Mix together sugar, cornstarch, and salt. Slowly add to boiling water, and cook, stirring frequently, until thick and smooth. Add some of the hot mixture to beaten egg, then stir back into pan with butter; cook 2 minutes longer. Remove from heat, and blend in lemon juice, grated lemon peel, and vanilla. Cool well before putting on cooled cheesecake.

Sour Cream Topping

2 cups commercial sour cream
2 tablespoons sugar
⅛ teaspoon salt

Combine sour cream with the sugar and salt, and spread over top of cooled cheesecake.

Chocolate Cheesecake: Prepare the basic cheesecake, but just before you turn it into the crumb-lined pan, add the following: 1 square (1 oz.) unsweetened chocolate, melted, and 1 teaspoon instant coffee powder. Bake and cool as above. If you want to be extra fancy, garnish top with puffs of whipped cream that's been marbled with chocolate sundae sauce, or use a vegetable peeler to make curls from unsweetened chocolate to garnish top.

Marbled Cheesecake: Prepare the basic cheesecake and divide the batter in half. Melt ½ square (½ oz.) unsweetened chocolate; blend into half the batter. Spoon alternate light and dark batters into the pan, then run a knife through to give marbled effect. Bake and cool as above.

Spiced Apple Cake

This moist, not-too-sweet cake goes well with any meal. Serve it plain or sprinkled with powdered sugar.

½ cup butter or margarine
1 cup firmly packed light brown sugar
2 eggs
½ teaspoon vanilla
2 cups all purpose flour, unsifted
1¼ teaspoons soda
½ teaspoon baking powder
1 teaspoon ground cinnamon
¼ teaspoon salt
1 container (8 oz.) spiced apple yogurt
½ cup finely shredded, peeled apple
½ cup chopped walnuts or pecans
Powdered sugar (optional)

Using an electric mixer, beat butter and brown sugar together until light and creamy. Add eggs and beat until fluffy; beat in vanilla. Combine flour with soda, baking powder, cinnamon, and salt; sift into the creamed mixture. Add yogurt and apple; mix just until blended. Stir in nuts.

Pour into a greased and floured 2-quart tube mold or 5 by 9-inch loaf pan. Bake in a 350° oven until a wooden pick inserted in center comes out clean (about 45 minutes for a tube mold, 60 minutes for a loaf pan).

Cool in pan 10 minutes; turn out on a rack to cool completely. If desired, sprinkle with powdered sugar before serving. Makes 10 to 12 servings.

Whipped Cream Pound Cake

Slices of this remarkably simple poundcake—made with whipped cream instead of shortening—are delicious plain or toasted.

1½ cups all-purpose flour (sift before measuring)
1 cup sugar
2 teaspoons baking powder
½ teaspoon salt
1 cup whipping cream
2 eggs
1 teaspoon vanilla

Sift flour again with sugar, baking powder, and salt. Whip cream until stiff; beat in eggs and vanilla. Add sifted dry ingredients and stir until thoroughly blended. Pour batter into a buttered and sugar-dusted 9 by 5-inch loaf pan. Bake in a moderate oven (350°) for 55 minutes or until cake just begins to pull away from edge of pan. Let stand for 10 minutes, turn out on a rack and let cool, or serve warm. Makes 12 to 14 servings.

Apricot Upside-down Gingercake

Fresh apricot halves make an attractive topping for this spicy gingercake. Serve warm, if you like.

7 tablespoons butter or margarine
⅓ cup firmly packed brown sugar
12 fresh apricots (about 1 lb.), pitted and halved
½ cup granulated sugar
1 egg
½ cup light molasses
½ cup milk
1½ cups all-purpose flour, unsifted
1 teaspoon each soda, ground cinnamon, and ground ginger
¼ teaspoon salt
Red candied cherry halves (optional)

Place 3 tablespoons of the butter in a round 9-inch cake pan and place in oven while it is pre-heating to 325°. As soon as butter is melted, remove pan from oven. Distribute brown sugar evenly over bottom of pan. Arrange apricot halves, cut side down, in a single layer over brown sugar.

In a large bowl, beat remaining 4 tablespoons butter with granulated sugar until creamy. Add egg, molasses, and milk; beat until blended. Stir together flour, soda, cinnamon, ginger, and salt. Add to creamy mixture, beating until blended.

Pour batter over apricot halves and bake in a 325° oven for about 1 hour, or until wooden pick comes out clean when inserted in center. Immediately invert onto serving plate. If you want, place a cherry half in the center of each apricot. Serve warm. Makes 6 to 8 servings.

Mediterranean Fruit Cake Ring

1 cup each dates, golden dried figs, and
  currants
½ cup candied cherries
1 cup coarsely grated or thinly sliced
  candied peels (citron, orange, and
  lemon)
1 cup coarsely chopped walnuts
½ cup flaked coconut
⅓ cup muscatel or white port wine; or
  pineapple, orange, or apple juice
¼ cup shortening
½ cup sugar
2 eggs, well beaten
1 cup all-purpose flour (sift before
  measuring)
½ teaspoon baking powder
1 teaspoon salt
½ teaspoon anise flavoring

Pit dates and clip stems from figs; cut these fruits into strips. Wash and dry currants. Halve the cherries. Combine all the fruits with walnuts, coconut, and wine; let stand several hours, or overnight.

Cream shortening and sugar together until fluffy. Add eggs, beating until well blended; stir into the fruit mixture. Sift flour again with the baking powder and salt into the fruit mixture. Add anise flavoring, and mix thoroughly into a stiff batter. Turn into a greased and floured ring mold (8½ or 9 inches in diameter), or into a greased and floured (or waxed-paper-lined) loaf pan (9 by 5 by 3 inches). Bake in a slow oven (275°) for 1¾ to 2 hours (2½ hours for loaf cake). Cool. Makes 5 pounds.

Purple Plum Kuchen

A creamy white cheesecake layer crowns the crimson plum filling.

Butter Pastry (recipe follows)
4 cups pitted, sliced purple prune plums
1¼ cups sugar
1½ teaspoons ground cinnamon
1 large package (8 oz.) cream cheese,
  at room temperature
3 eggs
¾ cup sour cream
1 teaspoon vanilla
½ teaspoon grated lemon peel

Arrange fruit on top of butter pastry and sprinkle evenly with ½ cup of the sugar and cinnamon. Bake in a 350° oven for 15 minutes. Meanwhile, beat cream cheese with eggs, sour cream, the remaining ¾ cup sugar, vanilla, and lemon peel.

Remove pastry shell from oven; pour cream cheese mixture into partially baked pastry shell. Bake for about 35 minutes longer, or until top is set in center when pan is jiggled. Cool, then chill well. Makes 9 servings.

Butter Pastry

1½ cups all-purpose flour, unsifted
¼ cup sugar
¼ teaspoon salt
½ cup butter or margarine
1 egg yolk

Combine flour, sugar, and salt. With your fingers, rub in butter until mixture is mealy; stir in egg yolk. Work dough into a ball and press evenly into bottom of a 9-inch-square baking pan. Bake in a 350° oven for 10 minutes.

Paskha

There are about as many recipes for Paskha as there are Russian cooks; this is an uncooked version, made from a few simple ingredients. (Baker's uncreamed cottage cheese can be found in most markets in the dairy case.) Decorate the finished cheesecake as elaborately as you wish with candied pineapple, finely chopped pistachio nuts, candied cherries, blanched almonds, strips of angelica, or swirls of colored butter frosting forced through a pastry tube.

1 vanilla bean (6 to 8 inches long)
2 cups (1 lb.) sweet butter, at room
  temperature
1¼ cups sugar
3 egg yolks
2½ lbs. (about 5 cups, packed)
  baker's uncreamed cottage cheese
1 cup whipping cream
½ cup finely chopped candied fruits
  (optional)

Split vanilla bean lengthwise and scrape out seeds, adding them to sweet butter. Add sugar to batter and beat until well blended; add egg yolks and mix thoroughly. Beat in cottage cheese, whipping cream, and candied fruits (optional).

Line Paskha mold, colander, or large wire strainer with clean muslin or several layers of cheesecloth and pour in cheese mixture. Fold cloth over cheese mixture surface, top with a plate, and put a heavy weight on plate. Place weighted mold in bowl or pan which will hold mold above drained liquid. Place in refrigerator for at least 24 hours. When ready to serve, remove weight and plate, lift off folds of cheesecloth, turn cheese mixture out onto serving plate, and lift off remaining cloth. Decorate with candied fruits as you wish. Cut into small wedges or slices. Makes 16 to 18 servings.

Caramel-Almond Topped Cake

You add melted butter to the batter to give a unique flavor to this cake.

2 eggs
¾ cup sugar
1¼ cups all-purpose flour (sift before measuring)
1¼ teaspoons baking powder
2 tablespoons evaporated milk or whipping cream
½ cup (¼ pound) butter or margarine, melted and cooled

Caramel-Almond Topping
¼ cup (⅛ lb.) butter or margarine
2 tablespoons evaporated milk or whipping cream
1 cup brown sugar, firmly packed
2 tablespoons flour
½ cup sliced almonds

Using your electric mixer, beat eggs and sugar together until thick. Sift flour again with baking powder into the egg mixture; mix until smooth. With your mixer set at low speed, beat in the milk and melted butter. Turn into a buttered 8 by 12-inch baking pan. Put in a moderate oven (350°, or 325° for a glass pan); bake about 30 minutes. Combine topping ingredients in a saucepan, and heat just to boiling. Spread the topping evenly over cake and put back in the oven 15 to 20 minutes, until caramelized. Let cool in pan. Makes 12 to 16 servings.

White Fruit Cake

This buttery, almond-perfumed white cake, unlike more moist fruit cakes, should be eaten freshly baked or only briefly aged. Chill thoroughly before slicing.

1 cup (½ pound) butter
1¼ cups sugar
3 cups all-purpose flour (sift before measuring)
¼ teaspoon salt
2 teaspoons baking powder
1 cup milk
1 teaspoon vanilla
½ teaspoon almond extract
1 cup chopped Brazil nuts
½ cup each chopped candied pineapple, sliced candied cherries, mixed candied fruits, and small pieces dried apricots
1 package (15 oz.) golden raisins
½ cup flaked coconut
6 egg whites

Cream together butter and sugar until fluffy. Sift flour again with salt and baking powder; set aside ½ cup. Combine milk, vanilla, and almond extract; add alternately with flour to creamed mixture. Dredge nuts, fruits, and coconut with the reserved ½ cup flour and stir into batter. Beat egg whites until they hold stiff peaks; fold into the batter.

Pour into 2 loaf pans (5 by 9-inch size) that have been buttered, lined with brown paper, and buttered again. Bake in a slow oven (275°) for 2 hours 30 minutes, or until wooden pick comes out clean when inserted in center. Have a shallow pan of water in bottom of oven. Cool in pans on wire racks. Remove from pans, and wrap individually in 2 layers of foil, sealing to make airtight. Freeze cakes, or age no longer than a month at room temperature, before eating. Chill before slicing. Makes 2 cakes.

Banana Coconut Cake

A buttery, broiled-on, banana-coconut topping makes this banana-flavored sheet cake an attractive dessert, as well as one that carries well to picnics, club meetings, or potluck dinners.

½ cup (¼ lb.) butter or margarine, at
  room temperature
2 cups cake flour (sift before measuring)
1 teaspoon each baking powder and
  soda
¾ teaspoon salt
1⅓ cups sugar
⅓ cup buttermilk
1 cup mashed ripe bananas
2 eggs
½ cup chopped filberts, pecans, or
  almonds
1 teaspoon vanilla
2 or 3 large yellow bananas, peeled

Coconut Topping

¼ cup butter or margarine, at room
  temperature
¾ cup brown sugar, firmly packed
¾ cup flaked coconut
1½ tablespoons milk

Place butter in a large bowl. Sift flour again into bowl with baking powder, soda, salt, and sugar. Blend well with butter. Mix together the buttermilk, bananas, eggs, nuts, and vanilla. Stir into the dry ingredients, mixing until all is moistened and blended thoroughly. Pour the batter into a buttered and flour-dusted 9 by 13-inch pan.

Bake in a moderately hot oven (375°) for 30 minutes or until cake just begins to pull from sides of pan. Let cool 5 minutes. Slice the whole bananas in thin lengthwise strips and arrange on top of the cake. Beat together ingredients for the coconut topping. Cover cake evenly with topping and broil about 4 inches from the heat until the top is lightly browned (about 2 or 3 minutes). Serve warm or cold. Makes 12 servings.

Raisin and Nut Cake

This layer cake is moist and rich, and chock full of ground raisins and nuts.

3 cups seedless raisins
1⅓ cups hot water
½ cup (¼ pound) butter or margarine
1 cup brown sugar, firmly packed
2 eggs, well beaten
2 cups all-purpose flour (sift before
  measuring)
1 teaspoon each salt and soda
1 teaspoon vanilla
1 cup coarsely chopped walnuts

Put the raisins through a food chopper with a medium blade; pour hot water over them and let stand until cool. Cream together the butter and sugar until fluffy; mix in the beaten eggs. Sift flour again with salt and soda. Add to the creamed mixture alternately with the raisin mixture. Stir in the vanilla and nuts. Turn into 2 well-greased 9-inch round cake pans; bake in a moderately hot oven (375°) for about 35 minutes, or until wooden pick comes out clean when inserted in center. Turn out of pans and cool thoroughly. Spread Brown Sugar Frosting between layers, and over top and sides. Makes 6 to 8 servings.

Brown Sugar Frosting

¼ cup butter, at room temperature
⅓ cup half-and-half (light cream)
1 cup brown sugar, firmly packed
1½ to 2 cups sifted powdered sugar

Combine butter, cream, and brown sugar. Bring to a boil; boil for 2 minutes, stirring. Remove from heat and beat in powdered sugar until mixture is of a good spreading consistency.

Strawberry Meringue Cake

½ cup (¼ lb.) butter or margarine
¾ cup sugar
2 egg yolks plus 1 whole egg
1¾ cups cake flour (sift before
  measuring)
¼ teaspoon salt
2 teaspoons baking powder
½ cup milk
1 teaspoon vanilla
Meringue Topping (recipe follows)
2 cups strawberries, sliced or whole,
  sweetened

Cream the butter; gradually add the sugar, beating until light and fluffy. Thoroughly beat in the egg yolks, then the whole egg. Sift flour again with the salt and baking powder. Add the flour alternately with the milk and vanilla to the creamed mixture. Pour into a well-greased 9-inch round cake pan. Bake in a moderate oven (350°) for 40 to 45 minutes. Turn out and cool on a rack. Scoop out a little of the center of the cake. Spread with Meringue Topping around top edge. Set into a 350° oven for 15 minutes, or until slightly browned. Cool. To serve, fill center with sweetened strawberries. Makes 8 to 10 servings.

Meringue Topping

2 egg whites
⅛ teaspoon salt
½ cup sugar

Beat egg whites with salt until stiff. Gradually beat in sugar, 1 tablespoon at a time, until glossy.

Savarin with Strawberries

For a spectacular dessert that can be baked ahead of time, try Savarin, soaked in syrup and centered with whipped cream and strawberries.

1 package yeast, active dry or
  compressed
¼ cup warm water (lukewarm for
  compressed yeast)
¼ cup milk
⅔ cup butter or margarine
2 tablespoons sugar
¾ teaspoon salt
4 eggs
2 cups all-purpose flour (sift before
  measuring)
Savarin Syrup (recipe follows)
1 pint heavy cream, whipped
2 cups strawberries (or other fruit),
  washed and sliced

Dissolve yeast in warm water. Heat milk to scalding and add butter; stir until butter melts, then add sugar and salt. Let cool to lukewarm (about 10°).

In large bowl of electric mixer, beat eggs, add the yeast mixture, then the milk mixture. Gradually beat in flour, mixing until batter is smooth. Pour batter into a well-buttered 8-cup Savarin mold.

Let rise in a warm place until almost doubled. Bake in a moderately hot oven (375°) for 35 to 40 minutes, until wooden pick comes out clean when inserted in center. While Savarin bakes, make Savarin Syrup.

With a fork, prick surface of the Savarin while it is still in the pan; turn out and prick the top. Baste several times with the syrup until the cake is thoroughly soaked. To serve, fill center of the Savarin with washed, halved fresh strawberries and whipped cream. Makes 6 to 8 servings.

Savarin or Baba Syrup

2 cups sugar
1 tablespoon grated orange peel
1 cup water or tea
½ cup rum or favorite liqueur

In a small saucepan combine sugar, grated orange peel and 1 cup water or tea. Bring to boil, then simmer over medium heat for 6 minutes; remove from heat and add rum or liqueur. Strain before using.

evaporated milk, slightly beaten eggs, vanilla, and lemon extract. Continue cooking, stirring, until custard mixture coats a metal spoon. Turn into crumb-lined pan. Sprinkle top with reserved crumbs. Bake in a moderately slow oven (325°) for 1 hour or until the point of a small knife inserted near center comes out clean. May be served when slightly warm or chilled. Makes 6 to 8 servings.

Caramel-Frosted Apple Cake

This apple cake is baked, frosted, and served from the same pan—an ideal dessert to carry to a picnic or potluck supper. It has a particularly wholesome flavor; a slightly coarse, teabread-like texture; and heavy, mellow, caramel frosting.

1¼ cups salad oil
½ cup sugar
2 eggs
2½ cups all-purpose flour (sift before
    measuring)
1 teaspoon each salt and soda
2 teaspoons baking powder
3 cups peeled and chopped apples
1 cup chopped pecans
Caramel Frosting (recipe follows)

Measure salad oil into a large bowl; add sugar and eggs and beat until creamy looking. Sift flour again with salt, soda, and baking powder. Add flour mixture in small amounts to oil, blending with each addition. Stir in apples and nuts. Spread batter evenly in a buttered 9 by 13-inch pan. Bake in a moderate oven (350°) for 50 to 55 minutes, or until cake just begins to pull from sides of pan. Let cool slightly and spread with frosting. Makes 12 to 16 servings.

Caramel Frosting

½ cup (¼ pound) butter
½ teaspoon salt
2 tablespoons evaporated milk
1 cup brown sugar, firmly packed
3½ cups sifted powdered sugar

Combine butter, salt, milk, brown sugar, and powdered sugar in a small saucepan and cook over medium-low heat, stirring until bubbling.

Apple Custard Torte

This heavy apple-laden filling develops from a custard that tastes very much like cream and sugar, slightly caramelized.

Crumb Crust

1 small box (6 oz.) zwieback, rolled into
    fine crumbs
½ cup sugar
1 tablespoon ground cinnamon
¼ cup (⅛ lb.) melted butter

Toss together zwieback crumbs, sugar, cinnamon, and melted butter. Reserve ½ cup for topping. Press remaining crumb mixture into bottom and sides of an 8 or 9-inch spring-form or removable-bottom pan.

Filling

7 large apples, peeled and sliced
6 tablespoons each sugar and butter
1 cup whipping cream
1 small can (6 oz.) evaporated milk
6 eggs, slightly beaten
1 tablespoon vanilla
1 teaspoon lemon extract

Combine in a saucepan apples, sugar, and butter. Cook over low heat until apples are soft. Stir in cream,

Orange and Cranberry Cake

2¼ cups all-purpose flour (sift before
    measuring)
1 cup sugar
¼ teaspoon salt
1 teaspoon each baking powder
    and soda
1 cup each chopped walnuts, diced
    pitted dates, and whole fresh or
    frozen cranberries
1 tablespoon grated orange peel
2 eggs, well beaten
1 cup buttermilk
¾ cup salad oil
1 cup each sugar and orange juice
Whipped cream (optional)

Sift flour again with the sugar, salt, baking powder, and soda. Stir in the nuts, dates, cranberries, and orange peel. Combine the eggs, buttermilk, and salad oil; stir into flour mixture until well blended. Pour into a well-greased 10-inch tube pan; bake in a moderate oven (350°) for 1 hour. Let stand about 15 minutes. Remove cake from pan and place on a rack over a pan. Heat the sugar with orange juice until dissolved; pour over cake, catching drippings and pouring back over cake several times. Set cake in a deep dish, and pour over remaining drippings; cover and refrigerate for at least 24 hours. Top with whipped cream, if you wish. Makes 10 to 12 servings.

Strawberry Shortcake

The term "short," of course, means rich with shortening. This recipe — it tastes a bit like Scotch shortbread, but with eggs in it — is really a short shortcake and a delicious companion to strawberries.

½ cup (¼ lb.) butter or margarine,
    at room temperature
1 cup sugar
2 eggs
2 cups all-purpose flour (sift before
    measuring)
½ teaspoon salt
1 teaspoon baking powder
3 to 4 cups sliced sugared fruit
About 1 cup whipping cream, whipped
    if desired

Put into a large bowl the butter, sugar, eggs, flour, salt, and baking powder. Using your hands, mix into a smooth dough. Line the bottom of a 10-inch round cake pan or an 8 by 12-inch baking pan with waxed paper; press in dough evenly. Bake in a moderate oven (350°) for 25 minutes, or until a light golden color. Cool slightly, turn from the pan, peel off paper, and carefully split into two layers. Fill with any sliced and sugared fruit and serve while still warm with whipped cream or thick unwhipped cream. Makes 6 servings.

Filbert Cake

Very finely ground filberts replace flour in this tender, moist cake. Grind the filberts as fine as cornmeal (use either the fine blade of a food chopper, a nut grater, or a blender).

½ pound (3 cups) shelled but
    unblanched filberts (about 3 pounds
    unshelled nuts)
10 egg yolks
¼ teaspoon salt
1 cup sugar
1 teaspoon vanilla
6 egg whites
Whipped cream or butter icing
    (optional)

Finely grind shelled filberts (or whirl a few at a time in blender). Beat egg yolks until very light. Add salt, sugar, and vanilla, and mix well; fold in the filbert meal lightly. Beat egg whites until stiff and fold into the mixture. Pour into a buttered and lightly floured 10-inch angel cake pan; bake in a moderately slow oven (325°) for 1 hour. Cool slowly, remove from pan, and serve as is, or with whipped cream or any butter icing. Makes 10 servings.

Chiffon Fruit Cake

This cake combines the richness of the standard fruit cake with the lightness of a cheesecake.

⅔ cup golden raisins, coarsely chopped
⅔ cup thinly sliced citron
½ cup each thinly sliced candied
    orange peel, candied cherries, and
    candied pineapple
½ cup light rum or sherry, or
    2 tablespoons rum flavoring with
    6 tablespoons water
3 tablespoons lemon juice
1½ teaspoons vanilla
½ teaspoon grated lemon peel
1½ cups coarse macaroon crumbs
1 tablespoon sugar
¼ cup (⅛ lb.) melted butter
½ cup sliced Brazil nut meats, chopped
    filberts, or pecans
1½ envelopes (1½ tablespoons)
    unflavored gelatin
½ cup milk
⅔ cup sugar
¾ teaspoon salt
3 eggs, separated
2 cups small curd cottage cheese
1 cup whipping cream

Combine raisins, citron, orange peel, cherries, and pineapple with the rum, lemon juice, vanilla and lemon peel. Let stand several hours or overnight.

Mix crumbs, the 1 tablespoon sugar, and butter. Press 1 cup of mixture into bottom of buttered 8 or 9-inch spring-form or removable-bottom pan. Add nuts to rest of crumbs; set aside.

In top of double boiler, mix together thoroughly the gelatin, milk, the ⅔ cup sugar, and salt. Beat egg yolks and add. Cook over hot water, stirring, for 5 to 10 minutes, or until mixture coats back of spoon. Remove from heat and blend in cottage cheese. Cool until mixture begins to jell (it should "mound" when spoonful is lifted). Beat egg whites until stiff; fold in. Whip cream until thick; fold in.

Carefully fold in rum and fruit mixture. Turn into crumb-lined pan. Sprinkle remaining crumbs and nut meats over top; chill in refrigerator until firm, about 4 hours or overnight. Makes 10 to 12 servings.

Pumpkin Pudding Chiffon Cake

You can make this chiffon cake with either granulated or brown sugar. If you use brown sugar, the crust will be very brown, so don't make the mistake of thinking the cake is burned before it has finished baking. It's very moist and tender—a delicious dessert with ice cream.

2 cups all-purpose flour (sift before
    measuring)
1½ cups sugar (part or all brown sugar
    firmly packed)
1 tablespoon baking powder
1 teaspoon each salt and ground
    cinnamon
¼ teaspoon ground nutmeg
⅛ teaspoon each ground ginger and
    cloves
½ cup salad oil
6 egg yolks
½ cup each canned or cooked pumpkin
    and water
1 cup egg whites (about 8 whites)
½ teaspoon cream of tartar
Powdered sugar or thin glaze (optional)

Sift flour again with 1 cup of the sugar, baking powder, salt, and spices into a large mixing bowl. Make a well in center of flour mixture and add oil, egg yolks, pumpkin, and water; beat until smooth. Combine whites and cream of tartar, beat to form soft peaks, and gradually whip in remaining ½ cup sugar to form stiff, glossy peaks.

Fold pumpkin mixture into egg whites and blend well. Pour into an ungreased 10-inch tube pan; bake in a moderately slow oven (325°) for 1 hour and 15 minutes, or until top springs back when lightly touched and cracks look dry. Invert pan (over a funnel) and let cake cool before removing from pan. Serve plain, or dusted with powdered sugar, or frosted with a thin glaze or icing. (You can also bake this cake in a 9 by 13-inch baking pan at the same temperature for 55 to 60 minutes.) Makes 10 servings.

Honey Chiffon Cake

Honey, coffee, and spices subtly flavor this springy chiffon cake.

1⅓ cups each *honey and hot strong
    coffee*
3½ cups all-purpose flour, unsifted
1 cup granulated sugar
2½ teaspoons baking powder
1 teaspoon each *soda and ground cinnamon*
⅛ teaspoon each *salt, ground cloves,
    and ginger*
¼ cup salad oil
4 eggs, separated
¼ teaspoon cream of tartar
Powdered sugar
Sliced almonds for garnish (optional)

Dissolve honey in hot coffee; let cool. Stir together flour, ½ cup of the granulated sugar, baking powder, soda, cinnamon, salt, cloves, and ginger. Make a well in flour mixture and add oil, egg yolks, and coffee-honey mixture; stir until smooth.

In a large bowl, beat egg whites and cream of tartar until foamy; add remaining ½ cup granulated sugar, a tablespoon at a time, beating until stiff and glossy. Pour egg yolk mixture, about a third at a time, over whites and gently fold in just until blended.

Pour into an ungreased 10-inch tube pan. Bake in a 350° oven for about 1 hour and 15 minutes, or until top springs back when lightly touched. Invert pan on a funnel and let cool completely. Remove from pan. Sprinkle with powdered sugar and garnish top with almonds, if desired. Makes 10 to 12 servings.

Powdered Sugar Pound Cake

After baking, this cake has a sugary, beige-colored crust and smooth interior.

1½ cups (¾ pound) butter or
    margarine
1 pound powdered sugar
6 eggs
1 teaspoon vanilla
2¾ cups cake flour (sift before
    measuring)

In a large mixing bowl, beat butter or margarine until creamy. Sift powdered sugar; gradually add to butter,

beating until mixture is light and fluffy. Beat in eggs, one at a time, beating well after each addition. Beat in vanilla. Gradually beat cake flour into creamed mixture. Pour into a greased and floured 10-inch tube cake pan. Bake in a slow oven (300°) for 1½ hours or until a toothpick inserted in the center comes out clean. Cool 5 minutes; turn out onto wire rack to cool thoroughly. Makes 10 to 12 servings.

Dark Fruit Cake

1 pound each *mixed candied fruits,
    candied pineapple, and candied
    cherries, chopped*
2 packages (15 oz. each) *golden
    raisins, coarsely chopped*
1 package (15 oz.) *raisins, coarsely
    chopped*
1 package (11 oz.) *currants, chopped*
1 pound pitted dates, coarsely chopped
1 cup each *white wine and orange juice*
8 eggs, beaten
1 cup each *firmly packed brown sugar,
    granulated sugar, and corn syrup*
2 cups salad oil
4 cups all-purpose flour (sift before
    measuring)
1 cup cake flour (sift before measuring)
4 teaspoons baking powder
3 teaspoons ground cinnamon
1 teaspoon ground allspice
2 teaspoons salt
2 cups plum jam
½ teaspoon soda
1 cup broken walnuts
2 cups broken pecans

Combine candied fruits, raisins, currants, and dates in a large bowl; pour wine and orange juice over fruits and let stand overnight. The next day, beat together thoroughly the eggs, brown sugar, granulated sugar, corn syrup, and salad oil. Sift flours together with baking powder, cinnamon, allspice, and salt. Fold into egg mixture alternately with plum jam blended with soda. Stir in fruits and liquid, and nuts. Pour batter into 2 well-greased and floured 10-inch tube baking pans. Bake in a moderately slow oven (275°) for 3 hours, with a pan of water in the bottom of the oven. (Or you can use 4 bread pans of 5 by 9-inch size, and bake at 275° for 2 hours 45 minutes.)

Cool on racks, remove pan, wrap cakes in foil, and seal in airtight containers. Age at least a week before serving. Makes about 12 pounds of cake.

Pies and Pastries

There are outstanding pies and pastries for all occasions here, from the exotic many-layered *baklava* of the Middle East to standard apple pie, made different and extra flavorful with a brushing of orange glaze. Beautiful and buttery, tissue-layered French pastries are explored by the simplest and most effective route. And for pie and tart fanciers, there is something for every taste—fruit, nut, chocolate, and ever so many more variations for fillings, some rich, some light. You bake some, refrigerate others.

Basic Flaky Pastry

There's not much to a pie crust—just flour, shortening, a little salt, and water—but the quality of this simple pastry is regarded as the measure of a cook's ability. It has to be good tasting, beautifully and evenly browned, short and flaky.

There are many methods for making good pie crust. Looked upon with special favor is the old-fashioned pie crust "like grandmother used to make." It calls for cutting in the fat, stirring in water to make a dough, and rolling out with no preliminary chilling (although this does no harm). You can use any solid shortening, lard, or butter. Butter does not make quite as tender and flaky a pastry, but some feel the flavor merits the exchange.

We have given proportions for making a single-crust pie and for a double-crust pie. The two-crust pastry dough can also be split evenly and used for two single-crust shells.

Fresh sweet cherries top this rich, smooth cheesecake (recipe, page 33).

Single crust for 9-inch pie

1 ⅓ cups all-purpose flour (sift before measuring)
¼ to ⅓ teaspoon salt
⅓ cup shortening
2½ to 3 tablespoons water

Double crust for 9-inch pie

2 cups all-purpose flour (sift before measuring)
½ teaspoon salt
½ cup shortening
5 to 5½ tablespoons water

Sift flour with salt into a bowl. Add half of the shortening. Cut into flour until mixture resembles cornmeal; use pastry blender or two knives. Add the remaining shortening and cut it into flour until the largest pieces are the size of small peas.

Sprinkle the smallest measure of water over flour, tossing lightly with a fork as you add the liquid. Stir vigorously in a circular motion, drawing the dough into a ball; add a little more water if mixture will not hold together. Pat into a ball and turn onto a lightly floured board. (For the two-crust pie, divide dough into slightly uneven portions, using the larger amount for the bottom layer; cover unrolled portion.)

Dust surface of dough lightly with more flour, and with your hand, pat into a flat round cake with smooth edges. With a rolling pin, roll out from center of dough to form a circle that extends at least 1¾ inches beyond outside rim of pie pan. (Roll top crust in the same manner, but circle need extend only 1¼ to 1½ inches beyond pan rim.) Do not stretch dough, always roll to make larger. If your circle of dough isn't shaping up as desired, push (do not fold) the edge back toward the center. While dough cake is still fairly small, turn occasionally and lightly flour beneath to prevent sticking.

Fold circle of dough gently in half and lift into the pie pan. Center and fit dough into pan, patting in place. Trim pastry edge evenly, leaving about ½ to ¾ inch overhang beyond rim. For single-crust pie, fold overhang under, crimp or flute edge decoratively with floured fingers, or press down with a floured fork. For double-crust pie, trim pastry edge evenly, leaving only about ¼ to ½ inch overhang beyond rim. Fill according to choice and place the top crust on surface. Trim edge of top crust, leaving about a ½-inch overhang. Tuck overhang in between edges of bottom crust and rim of pan. Crimp or flute edge firmly with floured fingers to seal, or press down gently with floured fork. Cut slits in top crust to let steam escape. Bake as directed in filled pie recipe.

To bake a single, unfilled crust, there are two methods to consider. The first is simply to prick the pastry shell liberally with tines of a fork before baking to allow steam to escape and prevent buckling of the crust. This method gives more even browning, but there is greater opportunity for the crust to be distorted by steam activity. The second method is to nest a large piece of foil, edges turned up to make a pocket, in the crust, making sure the foil does not cut into edges of crust. Fill with enough dry beans or rice to hold in place. This retains crust shape, but bottom does not brown as much as the rim. Bake in a hot oven (425°) for 12 to 14 minutes or until golden brown. Fill as desired.

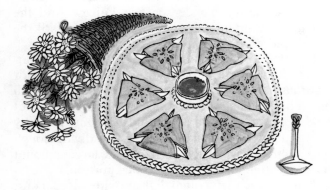

Basic Crumb Crust

1½ cups finely crushed graham cracker
  crumbs
⅓ cup sugar
⅓ to ½ cup melted butter or margarine

Combine crumbs with sugar and blend in melted butter or margarine. Press firmly onto bottom and sides of a 9-inch pie pan. Chill for 1 hour, or bake in a moderate oven (350°) for about 10 minutes to set the crust. The baked crust will be firmer.

Filbert Graham Crust: Substitute 1 cup ground filberts for ½ cup of the graham cracker crumbs. Mix remaining 1 cup cracker crumbs with nuts and sugar and blend in melted butter. Bake for 10 minutes in moderate oven to toast slightly.

Chocolate Graham Crust: Add 2 tablespoons of sweet ground chocolate to the melted butter before stirring into the cracker crumbs.

Cooky Crust: Substitute either vanilla or chocolate wafer crumbs, or gingersnaps, for graham cracker crumbs. Omit sugar included in the basic recipe.

Zwieback Crust: Substitute zwieback crumbs for graham cracker crumbs and use powdered sugar instead of granulated. Add a teaspoon of cinnamon if you wish.

Ready-to-eat Cereal Crust: Substitute crushed corn flakes, crisp rice cereal, or flaked wheat cereal for cracker crumbs.

French Apple Tart

A twice-baked, crunchy bottom crust and a once-baked, latticed top crust gives this pretty tart a unique place among the hundreds of recipes for "wonderful apple pies." You cook apple wedges in a white wine syrup, arrange in a baked pie shell, lace the top with your favorite pastry, and sprinkle on a sugar glaze.

Pastry for 2-crust 9-inch pie
5 large apples, peeled and cored
½ cup each dry white wine and water
1 cup sugar
1 tablespoon tapioca
1 teaspoon vanilla
½ teaspoon salt
Sugar

Use half of pastry to prepare a pastry shell for a 9-inch pie; bake in hot oven until lightly browned. Cut each apple into 8 wedges. Cook gently in syrup made by combining wine, water, sugar, tapioca, vanilla, and salt until almost tender (about 10 minutes). Turn into baked pie shell. Roll out remainder of pastry, cut into strips ½ inch wide. Arrange lattice over top; seal edges. Sprinkle with sugar. Bake in a moderate oven (350°) 15 minutes or until lattice is browned. Makes 6 to 8 servings.

Deep-Dish Almond-Apple Pie

The very deep filling layer for this pie combines the texture interest of crunchy almonds with fresh flavor touches of citrus and spices.

6 medium-sized apples, peeled and
    chopped
1 cup raisins
⅔ cup sliced almonds
1 cup sugar
½ cup orange juice
Juice and grated peel of 1 lemon
1 teaspoon ground cinnamon
¼ teaspoon salt
Pastry for 2-crust 9-inch pie

Combine chopped apples with raisins, almonds, sugar, orange juice, lemon juice and peel, cinnamon, and salt. Roll out ⅔ of pastry. Line an 8-inch square baking pan. Turn in apple mixture. Cover with top crust; seal edges; slash top. Bake in a hot oven (425°) 15 minutes. Reduce heat to 350°; bake 40 minutes more or until well browned. Makes 8 servings.

Shredded Apple Pie

Instead of the usual spices, this apple pie has flavors of lemon and orange predominating. It is both unusual and delicious.

Pastry for 2-crust 9-inch pie
1½ teaspoons grated lemon peel
1 tablespoon grated orange peel
¼ cup orange juice
2 teaspoons lemon juice
1½ tablespoons flour
1½ cups sugar
4 cups shredded cooking apples (about
    6 medium-sized apples)
2 eggs, well beaten
Whipped cream (optional)

Line a 9-inch pie pan with about half the pastry. In a large bowl, combine the lemon and orange peel with the fruit juices. Add the flour to the sugar and blend into the fruit juices. Peel the apples and shred quickly, using a medium-sized shredder. Add the shredded apples to the fruit juice and sugar. Stir in the beaten eggs. Pour the mixture into the pastry-lined pan. Arrange top crust or make lattice strips of the pastry. Seal the edges, making a fluted rim. Bake in a hot oven (450°) for 15 minutes. Reduce the heat to moderate (350°) and bake for about 30 minutes longer or until well browned. Serve warm or cold; top each piece with whipped cream, if you wish. Makes 6 to 8 servings.

Orange-Glazed Apple Pie

Addition of the sprightly flavor of orange gives an entirely different character to this otherwise rather typical double-crusted apple pie. The finishing touch is a thin orange glaze that you pour over the warm pie; as it cools, the glaze hardens slightly and makes a shiny surface.

Pastry for 2-crust 9-inch pie
5 cups peeled and thinly sliced apples
2 teaspoons flour
¾ cup brown sugar, firmly packed
¾ teaspoon ground cinnamon
¼ teaspoon each ground nutmeg and
  salt
2 teaspoons grated orange peel
2 tablespoons butter or margarine

Orange Sugar Glaze

¾ cup sifted powdered sugar
½ teaspoon grated orange peel
4 teaspoons orange juice

Line a 9-inch pie pan with about half of the pastry. Lightly toss apples with flour, sugar, cinnamon, nutmeg, salt, and orange peel and turn into pastry shell. Dot apples with the butter and cover with the remaining pastry, rolled thin. Seal edges of crust and make several slashes across the top of the pie. Bake in a hot oven (425°) for about 45 minutes, or until apples are tender and crust is well browned. Let pie cool 10 minutes. To make glaze, blend powdered sugar with grated orange peel and orange juice. Pour orange sugar glaze over top crust. Let cool slightly before serving, or chill. Makes 6 to 8 servings.

Apricot Pie

This fresh apricot pie can be served warm or cold.

Pastry for 2-crust 9-inch pie
3½ cups pitted, halved apricots
¾ cup sugar
2 tablespoons tapioca
1 tablespoon lemon juice
¾ teaspoon grated orange peel
  (optional)
Butter

Line a 9-inch pie pan with half the pastry. Arrange a layer of apricots on the pastry; sprinkle with about half of the sugar; arrange the remaining apricots on top; sprinkle with remaining sugar, tapioca, lemon juice, and orange peel (if used). Dot with butter; add top crust. Seal edges and slash top. Bake in a hot oven (400°) for about 40 minutes or until crust is golden brown. Makes 6 to 8 servings.

French Pear Pie

You sharpen the delicately flavored pears in this crumb-topped pie with orange juice concentrate.

4 large fresh pears
3 tablespoons thawed frozen orange
  juice concentrate
1 unbaked 9-inch pastry shell
½ cup sugar
Pinch of salt
¾ cup all-purpose flour, unsifted
⅓ cup butter or margarine
1 teaspoon ground cinnamon

Peel, core, and slice pears thinly. Toss lightly with the undiluted orange juice concentrate and arrange in the pastry-lined pan. Mix together the sugar, salt, flour, butter, and cinnamon until mixture is crumbly, and sprinkle over the pears. Bake in a hot oven (400°) for 40 minutes, or until the fruit is tender. Makes 6 to 8 servings.

Deep Dish Blueberry Pie

Spices, both mixed with the berries and sprinkled on the single top crust, point up the flavor of this berry pie.

1 cup sugar
2 tablespoons flour
¾ teaspoon ground cinnamon
¼ teaspoon ground nutmeg
⅛ teaspoon salt
3½ cups blueberries or huckleberries
1 teaspoon lemon juice
2 teaspoons butter or margarine
Pastry for 1-crust, 9-inch pie
2 tablespoons half-and-half (light cream)
2 teaspoons sugar
½ teaspoon ground cinnamon
1 cup whipping cream, whipped and
  sweetened

Mix together the 1 cup sugar, flour, ¾ teaspoon cinnamon, nutmeg, and salt; sprinkle over berries in a 1-quart casserole. Sprinkle with lemon juice; dot with butter. Roll out pastry and place over berries; flute edges, then slit pastry for steam to escape. Brush with cream and sprinkle with a mixture of the 2 teaspoons sugar and the ½ teaspoon cinnamon. Bake in a hot oven (450°) for 10 minutes; reduce heat to 350° and continue baking for 30 minutes longer or until well browned. Spoon into serving dishes and top with sweetened whipped cream. Makes 8 servings.

Pear Anise Pie

One spice, anise seed, blends with lemon peel and pears for a surprising harmony of flavors in this dessert pie.

Pastry for a 2-crust 9-inch pie
2 tablespoons butter or margarine,
  at room temperature
5 or 6 large fresh pears
⅔ cup sugar
3 tablespoons cornstarch
1 teaspoon whole anise seed
1 teaspoon grated lemon peel
1 teaspoon lemon juice

Line a 9-inch pie pan with about half the pastry. Spread 1 tablespoon of the soft butter over pastry and place it in the refrigerator while you prepare fruit. Peel, core, and slice pears into bowl. Blend sugar with cornstarch, anise seed, and lemon peel; mix lightly into pears, and turn into the pie pan. Sprinkle with lemon juice and dot with the rest of the butter. Adjust top crust, sealing edges well and cutting vents in top crust for steam to escape. Bake in a hot oven (425°) for about 15 minutes, then reduce temperature to 350°; bake about 20 minutes longer, until pears are tender. Cool. Makes 6 to 8 servings.

Note: You can glaze top of pie, when you take it from the oven, with mixture of ½ cup powdered sugar, 1 teaspoon lemon juice, 1 to 2 teaspoons water.

Creamy Rhubarb Pie

The amount of sugar in this recipe is variable because we have found rather widely differing preferences regarding sweetness in rhubarb pies.

1 egg, beaten
1 cup commercial sour cream or unflavored yogurt
1 to 2 cups sugar
½ teaspoon salt
3 tablespoons tapioca
1 unbaked 9-inch pie shell
3 cups chopped fresh rhubarb

Combine the egg, sour cream, sugar, salt, and tapioca in a bowl. Fill the pie shell with the rhubarb; pour the egg and cream mixture over rhubarb, and bake in a hot oven (425°) for 15 minutes. Reduce heat to 350° and continue baking for 30 to 35 minutes or until filling is set. Makes 6 to 8 servings.

Apricot Glazed Strawberry Pie

The bright red glaze on this strawberry pie is made with apricot purée that has been colored with red food coloring.

1 pound fresh apricots or 1 large can
   (1 lb. 14 oz.) whole peeled apricots
½ cup water
½ cup sugar (less for canned apricots)
½ teaspoon salt
¼ cup cornstarch
¼ cup water
Red food coloring
1 baked 9-inch pie shell
1 quart strawberries, halved
Whole strawberries, for garnish
Whipped cream, for garnish

Wash, halve, and pit fresh apricots or drain and pit canned apricots. If using fresh apricots, put in pan with the ½ cup water and bring to a boil; it is not necessary to cook canned apricots before puréeing. Remove from heat at once and press through a wire strainer or whirl in a blender to make a smooth purée. Return puréed apricots to saucepan and stir in sugar and salt; bring to a boil. Mix together the cornstarch and the ¼ cup water; gradually stir into the apricot purée and boil 1 minute. Stir in enough red food coloring to make it bright strawberry red. Allow mixture to cool.

   Spread about ¼ cup of the apricot mixture over bottom and sides of pie shell. Fill with the halved strawberries and cover evenly with the apricot glaze. Garnish top of pie with whole fresh strawberries and slightly sweetened whipped cream. Chill until serving time. Makes 8 servings.

Cranberry Pumpkin Pie

When you combine mellow pumpkin with tart cranberries in just the right proportions—as in this dessert—neither flavor is predominant. As a result it tastes like an entirely new and delicious fruit.

2 cups fresh or frozen cranberries,
   ground
1 cup sugar
¾ cup canned pumpkin
½ cup milk
½ teaspoon each ground nutmeg,
   ginger, and cinnamon
¼ teaspoon salt
2 eggs, slightly beaten
1 tablespoon melted butter or
   margarine
1 unbaked 9-inch pastry shell
1 cup whipping cream, whipped
Sugar to taste

Blend together cranberries and sugar. Mix together pumpkin, milk, spices, salt, eggs, and butter; add cranberry mixture. Pour into pastry shell and bake in a very hot oven (425°) for 45 minutes or until all the pie when slightly shaken is set, except for spot about 2 inches in diameter in the center. Cool. Top with whipped cream sweetened to taste with sugar. Makes 6 to 8 servings.

Nut-Top Pumpkin Pie

¾ cup brown sugar, firmly packed
½ teaspoon salt
¼ teaspoon each ground ginger and
   nutmeg
½ teaspoon ground cinnamon
1½ cups pumpkin, canned or cooked
   and mashed
3 eggs, beaten
1½ cups half-and-half (light cream)
¼ teaspoon maple flavoring
1 unbaked 9-inch pastry shell with
   fluted edge
¾ cup finely chopped walnuts or
   pecans
Maple whipped cream (recipe follows)

In a large bowl, mix together sugar, salt, ginger, nutmeg, cinnamon, pumpkin, and eggs. In a saucepan, combine half-and-half with maple flavoring, and heat to boiling point; stir into pumpkin mixture. Pour filling into pastry shell and sprinkle nuts over the top. Bake in a hot oven (400°) for 40 minutes, or until the soft spot in the center is about 1 inch in diameter. Cool and serve with maple whipped cream. Makes 6 to 8 servings.

Maple whipped cream. For each ½ cup cream used, flavor with 1 to 2 tablespoons brown sugar and ⅛ teaspoon maple flavoring. Whip.

Cherry Cream Cheese Pie

Because it is so easy to make and so good, this pie has enjoyed long-lasting popularity. It's delicious made with either cherry pie filling or blueberry pie filling.

1 small package (3 oz.) cream cheese
½ cup powdered sugar
½ teaspoon vanilla
1 cup whipping cream
Butter-crumb crust (below) or 1 baked
  9-inch pastry shell
1 can (1 lb., 5 oz.) prepared cherry pie
  filling (or 1 can blueberry pie filling
  with 1 tablespoon lemon juice)

Beat together until smooth the cream cheese, powdered sugar, and vanilla. Whip the cream until stiff and carefully fold into the cream cheese mixture. Turn into the prepared pie shell, spreading evenly. Spoon the pie filling evenly over top. Chill thoroughly before serving. Makes 6 to 8 servings.

Butter-Crumb Crust

1 cup all-purpose flour, unsifted
2 tablespoons powdered sugar
½ cup (¼ pound) butter

Blend together flour, powdered sugar, and butter just until crumbly. Turn into a buttered 9-inch pie pan, and pat evenly on bottom and sides of pan. Prick well with a fork. Bake in a hot oven (425°) for 8 to 10 minutes, or until lightly browned. Cool before filling.

Peach-Cantaloupe Pie

Pastry for 2-crust 9-inch pie
3 cups fresh peeled peach slices
1 cup thinly sliced cantaloupe
1 cup sugar
¼ cup all-purpose flour, unsifted
½ teaspoon salt
¼ cup sliced almonds (optional)
1 tablespoon butter or margarine

Line a 9-inch pie pan with half the pastry. Combine peaches with cantaloupe, toss with a mixture of the sugar, flour, and salt. Arrange fruit in the pastry-lined pan, sprinkle with nuts, dot with butter. Cover with top pastry; bake in moderate oven (350°) about 35 minutes. Makes 6 to 8 servings.

Summer Plum Pie

Choose tart, full-flavored plums for this spicy and colorful pie.

1 to 1½ cups brown sugar, firmly
  packed (or half brown, half
  granulated sugar)
¼ cup all-purpose flour, unsifted
¼ teaspoon ground cinnamon
¼ teaspoon ground nutmeg
Dash salt
½ teaspoon grated lemon peel
1½ tablespoons lemon juice
3 cups quartered, pitted plums
Pastry for 2 crust 9-inch pie

In a bowl combine the sugar (exact amount depends upon the tartness of the plums you use), flour, cinnamon, nutmeg, and salt. Stir in the lemon peel, lemon juice, and plums; mix until blended.

Roll out about ½ the pastry to fit the pie pan. Place pastry in pan and pour in the fruit mixture. Roll out the remaining pastry and cut into strips to make a lattice top, or use a plain pastry top if you prefer. Start baking in a very hot oven (450°); after 10 minutes, reduce oven temperature to 350° and continue baking for about 30 minutes. Serve warm or chilled. Serves 6 to 8.

Orange Chiffon Pie

Whipped cream and toasted, slivered almonds are optional garnishes you might use to embellish this tangy citrus pie.

1 envelope (1 tablespoon) unflavored
  gelatin
¾ cup sugar
Pinch of salt
1 cup hot water
3 eggs, separated
1 can (6 oz.) frozen orange juice
  concentrate
3 tablespoons lemon juice
1 baked 9 or 10-inch pastry shell
1 cup whipping cream, whipped
  (optional)
¼ cup slivered almonds, toasted
  (optional)

In the top of a double boiler, mix together the gelatin, ½ cup of the sugar, and the salt. Stir in the hot water and cook over boiling water, stirring, until gelatin dissolves. Beat egg yolks slightly and stir in gelatin mixture. Return to double boiler; cook, stirring, until mixture coats the spoon. Remove from heat, and stir in the orange juice concentrate and lemon juice; chill until it starts to congeal. Beat egg whites stiff; gradually beat in remaining ¼ cup sugar. Combine two mixtures; spoon into pastry shell; chill. Top with whipped cream and almonds, if you wish. Makes 6 to 8 servings.

Chocolate Mint Pie

Chocolate and mint are a perfect flavor blend. This attractive two-toned pie is an old favorite.

1 envelope (1 tablespoon) unflavored
  gelatin
¾ cup sugar
2 cups milk
3 eggs, separated
1 tablespoon cornstarch
2 squares (2 oz.) unsweetened chocolate
½ cup whipping cream
3 tablespoons crème de menthe or
  mint syrup
1 baked 9-inch pastry shell
Unsweetened chocolate for garnish

In the top of a double boiler, mix the gelatin and ½ cup of the sugar. Stir in the milk gradually and set over boiling water until the milk is scalded. Beat egg yolks with cornstarch until light. Gradually stir in some of the hot milk mixture. Return to top of double boiler and cook over boiling water, stirring, until thickened. Chill until it starts to congeal.

Beat egg whites until stiff; gradually beat in remaining ¼ cup sugar. Beat cream until thick. Melt chocolate. Beat chilled custard mixture until fluffy; fold egg whites, then whipped cream into the custard. Divide the mixture; fold melted chocolate into one half; blend mint into other half. Turn chocolate filling into the pie shell; chill 5 minutes. Top with the mint filling. Chill. For garnish, cut curling strips with a vegetable peeler from edge of a bar of unsweetened chocolate (at room temperature). Makes 6 to 8 servings.

Cranberry Chiffon Pie

1 can (1 lb.) jellied cranberry sauce
1 package (3 oz.) orange-flavored
  gelatin
1 tablespoon lemon juice
1 teaspoon grated orange peel
1 egg white
1 baked 8 or 9-inch pie shell
1 cup (½ pt.) heavy cream
Sugar to taste

Heat cranberry sauce to boiling, stirring constantly. Remove from heat, add gelatin and stir until dissolved. Add lemon juice and orange peel and chill until almost set. Whip with a rotary or electric mixer until fluffy. Beat egg white until it holds soft peaks and fold into gelatin mixture. Pour into the pie shell and chill until firm. Top the pie with sweetened whipped cream. Makes 6 to 8 servings.

Lemon Ribbon-Layered Meringue Pie

Ribbon layers of rich lemon butter and vanilla ice cream make this an unusual version of old-fashioned lemon meringue pie. Don't hesitate to freeze the meringue; the freezing period actually improves the meringue texture.

6 tablespoons butter
Grated peel of 1 lemon
⅓ cup lemon juice
⅛ teaspoon salt
1 cup sugar
2 eggs
2 egg yolks
1 quart vanilla ice cream
1 baked 9-inch pastry shell
3 egg whites
6 tablespoons sugar

To make the lemon-butter sauce, melt butter; add lemon peel, lemon juice, salt, and the 1 cup sugar. Slightly beat whole eggs with egg yolks, combine with the other mixture, and cook over boiling water, beating constantly with a whisk, until thick and smooth. Cool.

Smooth half of the ice cream in pastry shell; freeze. Spread over it half the cooled lemon butter; freeze. Cover with the other half of the ice cream; freeze. Top with remaining lemon butter; freeze. Beat egg whites until stiff, gradually beat in the 6 tablespoons sugar; spread meringue on pie. Place on a board, lightly brown in a very hot oven (475°). Serve immediately or freeze. Makes 6 to 8 servings.

Double Decker Pumpkin Ice Cream Pie

9-inch graham cracker pie shell
1 pint vanilla ice cream
1 cup canned pumpkin
¾ cup sugar
½ teaspoon each nutmeg, ginger, and cinnamon
½ teaspoon salt
½ pint (1 cup) heavy cream

Line the pie shell with ice cream (allow it to soften slightly), making a layer about ½ inch thick. Place in the freezer while preparing the pumpkin layer. Blend together the pumpkin, sugar, nutmeg, ginger, cinnamon, and salt. Whip cream until stiff and fold in. Spoon this filling over the ice cream-lined pie shell. Return to the freezer for at least 2 hours. To serve, remove from freezer and let stand at room temperature 5 minutes, then cut. Makes 6 to 8 servings.

Cherry Cheese Pie

Rich, smooth cheesecake and fresh sweet cherries combine perfectly to make this dramatic pie.

4 packages (3 oz. each) cream cheese
2 eggs
½ cup sugar
¼ teaspoon almond extract
1½ cups halved pitted sweet cherries (Royal Anne or Bing)
About 1½ cups whole or halved pitted cherries for top (Royal Anne or Bing)
⅓ cup cherry jelly, melted and cooled, for glaze
9-inch pastry shell, baked and cooled

Beat together cream cheese, eggs, sugar, and almond extract until smooth and fluffy. Pit and halve cherries and arrange over bottom of baked pastry shell. Pour cream cheese mixture over the cherries and bake in a moderately hot oven (375°) for 20 minutes. Cool on wire rack. When thoroughly cooled, arrange whole or halved pitted cherries on top and spoon on cherry jelly glaze. Cool thoroughly before serving. Makes about 8 servings.

Coffee Cream Pie

A garnish of chopped nuts tops this creamy pie. Their crunchy texture is a pleasing contrast with the smooth filling.

1 pint (2 cups) heavy cream, chilled
½ cup powdered sugar
3 tablespoons instant coffee powder
Pinch of salt
½ teaspoon vanilla
1 envelope (1 tablespoon) unflavored
   gelatin
¼ cup cold water
1 baked 9-inch pastry shell
About ½ cup finely chopped pistachios,
   filberts, macadamias, or almonds
   (optional)

In the large bowl of your electric mixer or another deep bowl, combine cream, powdered sugar, instant coffee powder, salt, and vanilla. In a small saucepan, soften gelatin in the cold water; then heat until gelatin is thoroughly dissolved; remove from heat.

Beat the cream mixture until it is thick. Gradually pour in the dissolved gelatin and continue beating until well blended. Turn the mixture into the baked pastry shell and chill for at least 1 hour before serving. Just before serving, sprinkle your choice of chopped nuts in the center of the pie, if you wish. Makes 6 to 8 regular servings, but you might want to cut small pieces of this rich pie.

Milk Chocolate Pie

This delicious milk chocolate pie is creamy and smooth and tastes like candy.

1 bar (14 oz.) milk chocolate
2¼ cups milk
2 tablespoons each cornstarch and flour
Pinch of salt
2 egg yolks, well beaten
1 tablespoon butter
1 baked 9 or 10-inch pie shell
Whipped cream, sweetened and flavored

Using a vegetable peeler, pare down the long side of the chocolate bar (it should be at room temperature) to make a few long curls to use for garnish; set these aside. Scald 2 cups of the milk in the top of a double boiler. Chop *all except 3 squares* of the remaining chocolate bar (the leftovers make good nibbles for anyone who can't wait until the pie is finished). Stir chopped chocolate into the scalded milk until melted. Blend the remaining ¼ cup milk with cornstarch, flour, and salt until smooth. Add to the chocolate mixture slowly; stir until thickened. Add some of the hot mixture to the egg yolks, then slowly blend this back into the hot mixture. Cook until thickened, remove from heat, add butter, and cool. Pour into the pie shell; chill. Top with whipped cream, garnish with the chocolate curls. Makes 6 to 8 servings.

Date and Banana Cream Pie

Sweet and chewy dates make a fine contrast for the tender bananas in this excellent version of the ever popular banana cream pie.

½ cup sugar
¼ teaspoon salt
3 tablespoons flour
1½ cups milk
2 eggs
1 tablespoon butter
1 teaspoon vanilla
4 medium-sized, brown-flecked
   bananas, peeled and sliced
1 baked 9-inch pie shell
1½ cups pitted, sliced dates
1 cup heavy cream, whipped

In the top of a double boiler, combine sugar, salt, and flour; blend in milk. Cook over boiling water, stirring occasionally, until thickened. Blend some of the hot mixture with eggs, then return to the pan and cook for 1 or 2 minutes more. Remove from the heat, stir in the butter and vanilla. Let cool slightly, then gently mix in the bananas. Pour about ⅓ of the cream mixture into the pie shell, top with about half the dates, then add ⅓ more of the cream mixture. Add the remaining dates (save a few for garnish) and the rest of the cream mixture. Chill. Spread the top of the pie with whipped cream and decorate with the reserved dates and a few additional banana slices if you wish. Makes 6 to 8 servings.

Pecan Cream Cheese Pie

This rich, beautiful pie is served chilled, and can be made a day in advance.

1½ cups graham cracker crumbs
¼ pound butter or margarine
⅓ cup finely chopped pecans
2 large packages (8 oz. each) cream
    cheese
1 cup sugar
½ pint commercial sour cream
2 tablespoons sugar
2 teaspoons vanilla
Pecan halves

Prepare pie shell by blending the cracker crumbs, butter, and pecans; press mixture into a 9-inch pie pan. Blend softened cream cheese with the 1 cup sugar until smooth and creamy. Spoon into shell, smooth out, and bake in a moderate oven (325°) for 20 minutes. Remove pie from oven and spoon mixture of sour cream, 2 tablespoons sugar, and vanilla evenly over the top. Return to oven, increase heat to 350°, and cook 10 minutes longer. Garnish with pecans. Chill in refrigerator before serving. Serves 12.

Date Chiffon Pie

This delicate, light filling is a change from the usual syrupy sweetness of date pie. But the fruit flavor comes clearly through the creamy chiffon fluff base. Be sure to mix the cut dates thoroughly through the gelatin sauce before you fold in the whipped cream and meringue.

1 envelope (1 tablespoon) unflavored
    gelatin
¼ cup cold water
1 cup milk
¼ cup sugar
2 eggs, separated
½ teaspoon salt
1 teaspoon vanilla
1 cup pitted fresh dates, cut into
    small pieces
1 cup heavy cream, whipped
2 tablespoons sugar
1 baked 9-inch pastry shell
Nutmeg
Dates for garnish

Soften gelatin in cold water. In top part of double boiler, beat together milk, the ¼ cup sugar, egg yolks, and salt. Cook over hot water, stirring constantly until mixture coats spoon. Stir in softened gelatin until dissolved. Chill mixture until partially set, stirring occasionally. Stir in vanilla and dates. Fold in whipped cream. Beat egg whites until foamy; gradually add the 2 tablespoons sugar, beating until stiff but not dry. Gently fold into date mixture. Pile into pastry shell. Chill until filling is set. At serving time, sprinkle top of pie with nutmeg, and garnish with a few date slices. Makes 6 to 8 servings.

Fresh Pineapple Pie

1 medium-sized pineapple
2 eggs
1½ cups sugar
2 tablespoons flour
1 tablespoon each *grated lemon peel and lemon juice*
Pastry for 2-crust 9-inch pie

Trim peel from pineapple, and core. Cut fruit in bite-chunks; you should have about 3 cups. Beat eggs with sugar, flour, grated lemon peel, and lemon juice; blend with pineapple. Line a 9-inch pie pan with pastry; fill with pineapple mixture. Cover with pastry to make top crust; seal rim and slash top. Bake in a hot oven (425°) for about 45 minutes, or until crust is brown. Cool before serving. Makes 6 to 8 servings.

Spicy Raisin Pie

¼ cup sugar
2 tablespoons cornstarch
½ cup light corn syrup
½ teaspoon salt
1 teaspoon cinnamon
¼ teaspoon each *nutmeg and cloves*
2 eggs, separated
1 cup unflavored yogurt
1 cup raisins
1 baked 8-inch pastry shell
⅛ teaspoon cream of tartar
Pinch of salt
4 tablespoons sugar

In the top of a double boiler, mix together sugar, cornstarch, corn syrup, salt, cinnamon, nutmeg, and cloves. Beat egg yolks and add. Stir in yogurt and raisins. Cook over hot water until thickened, about 20 minutes. Pour into baked pastry shell. Beat egg whites until foamy; beat in cream of tartar and salt. Add sugar, a tablespoon at a time, beating until stiff peaks form. While filling is hot, top with meringue. Brown in moderate oven (350°) about 12 minutes. Makes 6 to 8 servings.

Lemon Cheese Pie

Here's a lemon pie that is creamy like cheesecake.

Lemon crust

1 cup all-purpose flour (sift before measuring)
½ teaspoon salt
⅓ cup shortening
1 egg, slightly beaten
1 teaspoon grated lemon peel
1 tablespoon lemon juice

Sift flour again with salt into a bowl. Cut in shortening until fine. Combine egg with lemon peel and juice; sprinkle over flour mixture. Mix with a fork until the dough holds together. Roll out to fit a deep 9-inch pie pan. Flute edge, prick, bake in a hot oven (400°) for 12 to 15 minutes. Cool.

Lemon Cheese Filling

1¼ cups sugar
¼ cup cornstarch
1 cup water
1 teaspoon grated lemon peel
⅓ cup lemon juice
2 eggs, separated
½ cup (half of an 8 oz. package) cream cheese

Combine 1 cup of the sugar with cornstarch. Stir in water, lemon peel and juice, and egg yolks, beaten. Cook, stirring, until thick. Remove from heat; blend in softened cream cheese. Cool. Beat egg whites to soft peaks; gradually beat in remaining ¼ cup sugar. Fold into lemon mixture. Turn into pie shell. Chill. Makes 6 to 8 servings.

Bavarian Peach Pie

1¼ cups mashed ripe peach pulp
1 package (3 oz.) orange-flavored
  gelatin
¼ cup sugar
¼ teaspoon cinnamon
1 cup well-chilled evaporated milk
2 tablespoons lemon juice
1 baked 9-inch pastry shell
Sliced peaches

Whirl peach pulp in an electric blender or mash until fine. Pour off juice until pulp is about consistency of apple sauce. Heat pulp just to the boiling point; add the gelatin, sugar, and cinnamon, stirring until thoroughly dissolved. Chill until thick but not set. Combine evaporated milk and lemon juice in a well chilled bowl and whip until stiff; fold into gelatin mixture. Pile into baked and cooled pie shell; chill until set, at least 1 hour. Serve garnished with additional peach slices, if you wish. Makes 6 to 8 servings.

Note: To make Bavarian peach pudding, pile the peach and evaporated milk mixture into 6 to 8 individual dessert dishes instead of the pie shell. Garnish the puddings with peach slices at serving time.

Hawaiian Pear Pie

1 unbaked 9-inch pastry shell
1 tablespoon flour
1 can (8 or 9 oz.) crushed pineapple,
  drained
6 medium-sized firm ripe pears, peeled
  and sliced thinly
¼ cup butter or margarine
½ cup brown sugar
½ cup all-purpose flour, unsifted

Dust bottom of chilled pastry shell with 1 tablespoon flour. Fill with alternating layers of pineapple and pears. Crumble together butter, brown sugar, and ½ cup flour and sprinkle over fruit. Bake in a hot oven (400°) for 35 to 40 minutes or until crust and topping are nicely browned. Serve warm or cold. Makes 6 to 8 servings.

Quick Blueberry Pie

To give this simple but delicious pie a festive look, decorate the top with pastry scraps formed into a flower and embellish with a border of sweetened whipped cream.

2 cups frozen blueberries
  (unsweetened)
1 unbaked 9-inch pastry shell
¼ cup butter or margarine
1½ cups sugar
2 eggs
Grated peel and juice of 1 lemon

Pour berries into pastry shell. Mix together thoroughly the butter and sugar; beat in eggs. Add lemon peel and lemon juice to creamed mixture and blend well. Spread over berries. Bake in a moderate oven (350°) for 1½ hours or until top is browned. Cool at least 40 minutes. Decorate with whipped cream, if desired, and baked pieces of pastry scraps cut in fancy shapes. Makes 6 to 8 servings.

Peach Pie Alaska

2 cups peeled and sliced fresh peaches
Sugar (if necessary)
4 egg whites
¼ teaspoon cream of tartar
Pinch salt
½ cup sugar
1 baked 9-inch pastry shell
1½ pints hard-frozen vanilla ice cream

Sweeten peaches with sugar and then chill. Beat egg whites until foamy. Beat in cream of tartar and salt. Gradually beat in the ½ cup sugar, adding it a tablespoon at a time and beating after each addition until egg whites form stiff peaks. Arrange chilled peach slices evenly in bottom of cooled pie shell. Cover peaches with slices of hard-frozen vanilla ice cream. Quickly spread meringue over ice cream and peaches, being careful to cover them well at edges. Bake in a hot oven (425°) until meringue is a delicate brown, about 4 minutes. Makes 6 to 8 servings.

Fresh Coconut Pie

You can gild this pie, if you wish, with thin slices of navel oranges. Instead of fresh coconut and milk, you can use 1½ cups frozen coconut milk, thawed.

1¼ cups milk
1 cup grated fresh coconut, well packed
2 eggs, separated
⅔ cup sugar
1 teaspoon cornstarch
1 envelope (1 tablespoon) unflavored
 gelatin
Dash of salt
1 cup heavy cream, whipped
1 teaspoon vanilla
About ⅓ cup flaked coconut, toasted
Thin slices navel orange (optional)
9 or 10-inch baked pie shell

Heat milk to scalding; pour over coconut and let stand for about 1 hour. Put through a fine wire strainer, pressing to extract all the liquid; discard the coconut. Beat egg yolks slightly, then beat in the coconut-flavored milk. In a pan mix sugar, cornstarch, gelatin, and salt; blend in egg-milk mixture. Cook over low heat, stirring, until thickened. Chill. When set, beat with electric mixer; fold in whipped cream and vanilla. Fold in egg whites that have been beaten until they hold soft peaks. Pour into pie shell; chill several hours. Garnish top with toasted coconut and orange slices, if you wish. Makes 6 to 8 servings.

Macadamia Nut Pie

This luxurious confection-like pastry is simply a revision of the old formula for the South's famous pecan pie; it's a taste variation—well worth investigating.

If you like to gild the lily, try topping wedges of the pie with scoops of a good vanilla ice cream.

One jar of macadamias, the 7-ounce size, is enough to make this pie; but if you can get the broken or chopped macadamias, sometimes available in food specialty shops, they are a more economical choice.

3 eggs
⅔ cup sugar
1 cup light corn syrup
1½ cups chopped macadamias (if the
 macadamias are unsalted, add ½
 teaspoon salt)
2 tablespoons melted butter
1 teaspoon vanilla
1 unbaked 8 or 9-inch pastry shell

Beat eggs with sugar and corn syrup. Stir in the nuts; add butter and vanilla, and blend well. Pour mixture into pastry shell. Bake in a moderately slow oven (325°) for 50 minutes or until crust is golden and center of pie is set; test by shaking gently. Let cool and chill. Makes 8 to 10 servings.

Baklava

Baklava, with its two dozen and more flaky layers filled with almonds, is perhaps the most famous Middle Eastern delicacy. Many restaurants and coffee houses serve it as a special dessert. If you start with prepared *fila* dough, this exotic pastry is fairly easy to make. One-pound boxes of these paper-thin dough sheets, neatly folded, are available in Greek food shops; if you are unable to buy the fila, you can make the dough according to recipe next page.

1⅓ pounds shelled almonds
⅔ cup sugar
Grated peel of 1 lemon or small orange
1 pound fila (1 commercial package or
 1 recipe fila, below)
1 cup (½ pound) melted butter
Cinnamon
Whole cloves
⅓ cup each sugar and water
1⅓ cups honey

Blanch, toast, and grate or finely chop the almonds; mix in the sugar and grated lemon peel. Spread some of the melted butter in a 9 by 13-inch baking pan and arrange 1 sheet fila in bottom, letting it hang over the edges of the pan an inch or two. Spread with butter and top with fila until you have 8 sheets of buttered fila in pan, each lapping over the edges. Spread with melted butter, sprinkle with cinnamon, and then sprinkle with about one-fourth of the almond mixture.

Fold in 1 layer of the overlapping sides, enclosing the nut layer. Top with 3 more layers of fila cut or torn to fit size of pan, buttering each one. Sprinkle generously with the nut mixture and again enclose, folding in the edges of one fila sheet. Repeat 3 buttered layers of fila topped with a nut layer, until you have at least 4 almond layers altogether, each enclosed in fila. Add 5 more fila layers, each buttered; sprinkle top with cinnamon. If any fila is still overlapping the sides, fold it back over the top.

Cut partially (into the first nut layer) diagonally across the pan, making diamonds about 1 inch wide and 1½ inches long. Stick a whole clove in the center of each diamond. Bake in a slow oven (300°) for 1 hour. Meanwhile cook together the sugar and water for 10 minutes; stir in honey and let cool. When you remove baklava from the oven, cut through completely, and while it is still hot, pour over the cool honey syrup. Makes 50 pieces.

Fila Dough

4 cups all-purpose flour, unsifted
1 teaspoon salt
About 1 cup water
6 tablespoons olive oil

Sift flour with salt; mix in enough water to make a soft ball. Knead in olive oil; knead until smooth. Let sit for 30 minutes. Divide dough into 16 equal portions. Using an extra long rolling pin or broomstick, roll out each portion of dough on a floured board until it is paper thin and about 16 by 24 inches. Makes 16 sheets of thin fila dough.

Puff Paste

If you've ever eaten a crisp, golden, sugar-glazed and cream-filled "French pastry," you've doubtless marveled at its buttery yet light and flaky composition. The French call such pastry, with its multiple, tissue-thin layers, *pâté feuilletée.* We call it puff paste. It can be used as the base for innumerable pastries.

1 pound butter
3⅓ cups all-purpose flour (sift before measuring)
1 teaspoon salt
1 cup ice water

Remove butter from the refrigerator. Sift flour again with salt into a bowl. Add ice water, a little at a time, mixing thoroughly with a fork. Dough will be very stiff. (If necessary, add a few more drops of water.)

Knead dough on an unfloured board until smooth, shiny, and elastic; this takes about 5 minutes. Place on a lightly floured board, and cover with the bowl. Let stand 20 to 25 minutes. (This is important: Dough is manageable after the waiting period.) This is called the *detrempe.*

On an unfloured board, roll the detrempe into a rectangle about 5 by 20 inches. Place the butter in the center of the rectangle. (Butter should be firm but not hard. If it is too soft, it will ooze out from between the layers of dough; if too hard, it will break through the pastry and ruin it. It will have the right consistency at about 50°.) Enclose by bringing one side of the detrempe over butter; press outside edges together to seal securely. Fold other side over and seal edges. The package of butter thus sealed in dough is called a *pâton.* (If butter seems soft, chill for 5 minutes.)

Place pâton on a lightly floured board. Hold rolling pin in both hands, using it to pound and flatten pâton slightly. (Don't pound too zealously, although dough will take more abuse than you might suspect.) Working carefully, but as quickly as possible, roll the pâton into a square-cornered, straight-sided rectangle of uniform thickness; make rectangle three times as long as it is wide and not less than ⅜-inch thick. (It is easier to maintain a rectangular shape, and there is less chance of breaking the pastry, if you roll from edges of pâton toward the center.) You should be able to see the butter spreading evenly under the pastry as it is rolled. If the pastry should tear, dust damaged section with flour.

Fold rectangle into thirds to form a three-layer square, with all edges and corners meeting exactly. This completes the first "turn" (you will make six turns in all). For the remaining five turns, follow this simple procedure:

Place folded dough on a lightly floured board, with one of the open edges toward you, the folded edges at the sides. Roll and fold as you did for the first turn. After the second and fourth turns, make depressions in dough with your fingertips (not fingernails) to remind you of the number of turns you have made; wrap pastry in waxed paper, then in a damp cloth, and refrigerate for 15 minutes or until pastry is about 50° throughout.

(If at any time the butter seems too soft to roll well, chill for about 5 minutes; or if it tends to break through the pastry, let it stand several minutes at room temperature before you begin rolling.)

When you have finished the sixth turn, the pastry is ready to use.

Puff paste wrapped in waxed paper, foil, or clear plastic wrap will keep four or five days in the refrigerator; or it can be frozen for six to eight months. Part of the pastry may be used immediately and the remainder frozen.

Papillons (Butterflies)

Make two additional turns (seventh and eighth) with one recipe quantity of puff paste on a sugared board, sprinkling pastry with 2 or 3 tablespoons sugar before folding each time. Roll ⅛-inch thick. Cut in strips 2 inches wide and of equal length. Stack 4 strips together, brushing each layer with water and sprinkling lightly with sugar. Using the edge of your hand, a dowel, or handle of a wooden spoon, press each strip firmly in the middle, lengthwise, making strip slightly thinner in that portion. Cut in ½-inch-long pieces. Then give each piece a half-twist in the middle (center crease makes this possible). Arrange on an ungreased baking sheet, with several inches between butterflies. Chill for 30 minutes. Bake in a hot oven (400°) for 8 minutes; reduce heat to slow (300°) and bake until nicely browned, 8 or 10 minutes (take care not to burn). Makes about 4 dozen.

Tresses (Braids)

Roll puff paste ⅛ inch thick on a sugared board. Cut in ⅜ to ½-inch-wide strips. Braid 3 together; cut to desired lengths. Brush with 1 egg beaten with 1 tablespoon water. Bake as directed for Papillons, above.

Couques or Langues De Boeuf

These are small, sugar-glazed ovals of puff paste, split and filled with flavored creams. They can be made with scraps (see recipe for Petite Bouchées).

On a sugared board, make an additional (seventh) turn with puff paste. Roll ⅜-inch thick. Cut in small plain or fluted rounds. Then, with one stroke of the rolling pin, form each into an oval. Place on an ungreased baking sheet. Chill for 15 minutes. Bake in a hot oven (400°) for 8 minutes; reduce heat to moderate (350°) and bake 8 minutes longer, or until nicely browned (take care that they do not burn). Cool. Split by lifting off top half or by dividing in three layers. Just before serving, sandwich together with sweetened whipped cream, flavored to taste with rum or rum flavoring.

Petites Bouchées

These thimble-sized pastry shells make flaky dessert morsels. Fill them with a bit of jelly or whipped cream. You can make them with scraps left from cutting out larger pastries.

Roll puff paste ⅛ inch thick on a lightly floured board. (When using scraps, arrange so that each piece is lying flat and overlapping the one next to it; roll all together. Fold in thirds to form straight sides; roll again.) Cut in 1-inch circles. Score all of the circles (cut almost through, but not quite) with a ½-inch cutter. Place on a baking sheet lined with a single layer of brown paper: chill. Bake in a very hot oven (450°) for 10 minutes or until brown. Remove centers and fill as desired.

Palmiers (Palm Leaves)

These crisp, sweet pastries are cut so that they fan out when baking. Be sure to allow plenty of room between them.

Make an additional (seventh) turn with one recipe quantity of puff paste on a sugared board, sprinkling the pastry with about ¼ cup sugar before folding and rolling. Now roll puff paste in a rectangle twice as long as it is wide and ⅛ to ⅜-inch thick. (The thicker the dough, the bigger the palm leaves will be.) Fold ends in to meet in the middle (this makes a square). Then roll just enough to flatten slightly. Sprinkle with sugar (about ¼ cup), then fold the folded edges in again to meet in the middle; flatten slightly. Now fold in half lengthwise, as if you were closing a book. Press firmly. Cut the dough in ¼ to ⅜-inch slices.

Arrange on an ungreased baking sheet, with 3 or 4 inches between palm leaves. Chill for 15 minutes. Bake in a hot oven (400°) for 8 minutes; turn palm leaves over and bake about 8 minutes more. Take care that the sugar doesn't burn.

Cornets (Horns)

Cone-shaped metal forms (available at bakery supply houses) or cones made of heavy foil support the shapes of these handsome pastries as they bake. Fill with flavored whipped cream.

Roll one recipe quantity of puff paste ⅛-inch thick on a lightly floured board. Using a ruler and sharp knife, cut pastry in strips ½ to ¾-inch wide and about 18 inches long. Starting at small end of the form, spiral each with a dough strip, letting each row overlap the one below by ¼ to ⅜ inch. Do not extend dough over the wide end of form. Moisten end and pinch firmly to anchor pastry. Place, joined side down, on a baking sheet lined with a single layer of brown paper; let chill. Brush with 1 egg beaten with 1 tablespoon water. Bake in a hot oven (400°) until nicely browned, about 25 minutes. Cool slightly; remove forms. If you like crisper pastries, return cornets to a moderate oven (350°) for about 5 minutes. Cool. Just before serving, fill with sweetened whipped cream flavored with rum, finely chopped nuts, or glacéed fruits. Makes about 2 dozen pastries.

To make cone forms: Fold extra-heavy aluminum foil double thickness in 9 or 10-inch squares. Fold each square diagonally to form a triangle. Roll into a cone, leaving a small opening at the small end. Fold top over to make foil cone firm.

Custards, Puddings, and Soufflés

Custards and soufflés, despite their many variations, are specific kinds of rather remarkable desserts in which eggs play an essential role to create the respective creamy or airy textures. A pudding might be the name of any sweet that is boiled, baked, steamed, or chilled.

THE PERFECT CUSTARD

Custards, stirred or baked, spicy or sweet, hot or cold, are so flexible in character that they suit any menu. When the demand is for a spectacular dessert, a flaming flan provides the drama; if the emphasis is on gourmet dining, then crème brûlée makes a fitting climax. And paired with fresh fruits and berries, a simple baked custard makes a refreshing summertime dessert that deserves frequent encores.

You'll find perfect custards easy to make if you follow these few principles of custard cookery. Beat mixtures only enough to blend completely; avoid creating a frothy layer. Cook stirred custards over hot—never boiling—water, stirring frequently with a spoon. A stirred custard is done when the mixture coats the back of a metal spoon smoothly, and when the watery appearance changes to a velvety opaque quality. The greater the proportion of eggs to milk, the heavier the coating will be.

Baked custards should always cook in an insulating bath of hot water. When you set the oven to preheat, place a pan of water in the oven—the pan should be large enough to hold the dish for the custard, and the water should be of a depth to surround the lower half of the custard mixture.

Serve Strawberries with Russian Cream (recipe, page 50) on top of crisp wafer cookies.

The most effective test to determine when a baked custard is done is to touch the surface (about in the center) with the back of a small metal spoon, and push the spoon to one side. If the crust clings and a clean crack about ⅜ inch deep forms, the custard is done. If the custard is soupy, or breaks indecisively, bake a while longer. If you bake the custard a day ahead, but want to serve it from another dish, cook in baking dish, cover, and refrigerate overnight. To facilitate removal from dish, set in warm water for about five minutes before inverting to release onto serving container.

WHEN PREPARING A SOUFFLÉ . . .

One of the most fascinating of all desserts is the delicate, airy soufflé; and it is not difficult to make, despite rumors to the contrary. It does fall, however, this being its natural behavior, and must be served immediately when it comes from the oven. Here are a few rules worth noting: The sauce must be the consistency of thick white sauce. The egg whites should be whipped just to the point where they hold short, distinct, moist-looking peaks. Folding whites with sauces should be done in two steps, with the first addition of whites blended thoroughly, and the remainder as thoroughly as you like (you can create a marbled effect by only partially blending in the second addition of whites). A soufflé dish helps the mixture attain the classic stand-out-of-the-dish look, but it is not an essential utensil. You can use any container of the proper capacity. The dish should be buttered, and dusting with sugar is a nice touch. Fill the dish at least three-quarters full for the soufflé to look its best. When the soufflé is done, it feels firm when lightly tapped, and the cracks look fairly dry. You can leave a baked soufflé in the oven without disaster for as long as five minutes.

ESSENTIALS FOR STEAMED PUDDING

Of all the puddings—those like cakes, cobblers, ones stiffened with gelatin or cooked and thickened or made from cereals—the steamed pudding requires the most equipment. Molds and steamers simplify the preparation of steamed puddings, but if you lack conventional steaming equipment, you can improvise easily. Ring molds, tall juice cans, casseroles, and coffee cans can work as molds if they are covered tightly. For a steamer, use any deep kettle with a tight-fitting cover. Place a vegetable steaming basket, a perforated pie pan, or a trivet in the kettle; pour in hot water until it comes up to the makeshift stand. When the water is boiling, place the filled mold in the basket (or on the trivet), cover the kettle, and keep the water boiling gently through the entire cooking period. If it is necessary to add more liquid to the kettle during the cooking, refill with boiling water.

Grand Marnier Soufflé

4 tablespoons each *butter or margarine and all-purpose flour, unsifted*
1 cup light cream
Dash salt
6 eggs, separated
¾ cup sugar
Grated peel of 1 orange
¼ cup Grand Marnier
Whipped cream
Grand Marnier

In a saucepan melt butter and blend in flour. Stir in cream and salt; cook, stirring, until thickened. Remove from heat. Beat in yolks, ½ cup of the sugar, orange peel, and the ¼ cup Grand Marnier. Whip whites until they hold soft peaks, then beat in remaining sugar until they hold short distinct peaks. Fold half the whites thoroughly into sauce; then fold in the remaining whites as thoroughly as you like.

Pour into a buttered and sugar-dusted 2-quart soufflé dish; fit a lightly buttered foil collar around dish (it should extend about an inch above rim). Bake in a moderately hot oven (375°) 15 minutes, then remove collar. (Do not remove from oven.) Continue baking for 20 to 25 minutes. Over each serving, spoon whipped cream flavored to taste with Grand Marnier (or flame each serving with a spoonful or so of the warmed liqueur). Makes 6 servings.

Variations: You can flavor this soufflé with Cointreau or curaçao instead of the Grand Marnier; or you can omit the orange peel and flavor the soufflé with Kahlúa or crème de cacao or other favorite suitably flavored liqueur.

Zabaglione

12 egg yolks
¼ cup sugar
1½ cups Marsala wine

Beat egg yolks with sugar until very light and thick. Heat Marsala wine. Put the egg mixture in the top of a double boiler over hot water; add the Marsala gradually, beating constantly with a rotary beater. Cook, beating, until thick and hot. (To avoid curdling do not allow water to boil.) Pour into heated sherbet or wine glasses and serve at once. Makes 6 to 8 servings.

Almond Crusted Custard

Nut meats float to the surface and form a crunchy topping on these individual rum-flavored custards.

¾ cup egg yolks (11 or 12)
½ teaspoon salt
⅓ cup sugar
½ teaspoon rum flavoring
3 cups light cream or milk
½ cup sliced almonds or Brazil nuts

Beat egg yolks with salt, sugar, rum flavoring, and cream. Pour into 6 custard cups (6-oz. or ¾-cup size); sprinkle with nuts. Set in a pan of water half the depth of custards. Bake in a moderate oven (350°) until custard tests done in center, about 35 minutes. Serve warm or cold from custard cups. Makes 6 servings.

Mousse au Chocolat

Thin shells of chocolate encase creamy chocolate mousse for this rich and frankly fancy dessert. It looks as if it could be produced only by a master chef, yet it is really very easy to make.

½ pound candy-dipping chocolate
 (or ⅓ pound bulk milk chocolate and
 ⅓ cup semi-sweet chocolate chips)
1 package (6 oz.) semi-sweet chocolate
 chips
1 square (1 oz.) unsweetened chocolate
6 eggs
Pinch salt

To make the chocolate cases, heat candy-dipping chocolate in the top of a double boiler until partially melted. Remove from heat and stir until entirely melted. Using a ½-inch artists' brush, paint the inside of 8 paper baking cups with the chocolate, keeping thin and evenly coated. Bring the chocolate to the top of the cups but do not allow it to run over the edges. Arrange on baking sheets and chill. When completely hardened, carefully peel away the paper, leaving little fluted chocolate cups. These may be kept in the freezer until used, but be sure to pack them carefully; it is a good idea to put each one in a fresh baking cup.

To make the filling, melt the semi-sweet chocolate chips and unsweetened chocolate. Beat eggs with salt until very thick and light; fold into the melted chocolate. Mix well and divide among the chocolate cases. Chill in the refrigerator until it is time for dessert. Makes 8 servings.

Mocha-Pecan Flan with Coffee Sauce

Decorate this flan with side and top borders of pecan halves and maraschino cherries on top. Flame with rum or brandy. Serve with a coffee sauce or spoon crème de cacao over serving wedges.

5 eggs
½ cup sugar
⅛ teaspoon salt
1½ teaspoons instant coffee powder
1 tablespoon cocoa
1⅔ cups milk or light cream
1 teaspoon vanilla
Pecan halves and maraschino cherries
3 tablespoons rum or brandy (optional)

Beat together the eggs, sugar, salt, instant coffee, and cocoa. Scald milk and beat immediately, along with vanilla, into egg mixture until blended. Pour into a buttered 8-inch round cake pan; place in ½-inch hot water and bake in a moderate oven (350°) for about 25 minutes or until done. Cool to room temperature. Run a knife around edge; turn out on a serving plate; garnish with pecans and maraschino cherries. Chill until just before serving.

To flame, heat 3 tablespoons dark rum or brandy until it begins to steam. Ignite and pour over flan. Cut into serving wedges. Pass Coffee Sauce or crème de cacao. Makes 8 to 10 servings.

Coffee Sauce

½ cup sugar
¾ cup hot, strong coffee
1 tablespoon cornstarch
2 tablespoons water
1 tablespoon butter
Dash salt
½ teaspoon walnut flavoring
¼ cup chopped walnuts

Place sugar in a small, heavy frying pan and melt slowly over low heat until it turns a light amber. Add coffee; stir until blended. Dissolve cornstarch in water; stir into sugar-coffee mixture and cook until thickened. Add butter, salt, walnut flavoring, and chopped walnuts. Pass to spoon over flan. Makes 1 cup.

Steamed Pumpkin Pudding with Satin Sauce

½ cup shortening (part butter, if
    desired)
1 cup brown sugar, firmly packed
¼ cup granulated sugar
1½ teaspoons salt
½ teaspoon each cinnamon and
    nutmeg
¼ teaspoon ginger
2 eggs, beaten
⅔ cup chopped Brazil nuts, pecans,
    or walnuts
2 cups all-purpose flour (sift before
    measuring)
1½ teaspoons baking powder
¼ teaspoon soda
¾ cup pumpkin, canned or cooked
    and mashed
¼ cup commercial sour cream or
    light cream

Cream together until blended the shortening, brown sugar, granulated sugar, salt, and spices. Add eggs and beat well. Stir in nuts. Sift flour again with baking powder and soda. Add flour to creamed mixture alternately with pumpkin and sour cream or light cream; mix well after each addition.

Turn batter into a well-greased 2-quart mold and cover tightly. Set mold in boiling water—water should be kept at a level that covers the bottom half of the mold. Steam in continuously boiling water for 2 hours. Let pudding stand for 5 minutes before removing from mold. Serve hot with cold Satin Sauce. Makes 10 to 12 servings.

Satin Sauce

1 egg
⅓ cup melted butter or margarine
1½ cups sifted powdered sugar
1 teaspoon vanilla
¼ teaspoon nutmeg
1 cup heavy cream, whipped

Beat egg until frothy, then beat in melted butter or margarine, powdered sugar, vanilla, and nutmeg. Carefully fold whipped cream into egg and sugar mixture. Refrigerate until ready to use. Stir to blend just before serving.

Cherry Bran Pudding

While this fruit dessert bakes, the cherry juice thickens into a smooth sauce.

1 can (1 lb.) pitted sour cherries
Water
¾ cup sugar
3 tablespoons butter or margarine
½ cup shredded bran cereal
¾ cup all-purpose flour (sift before
    measuring)
1 teaspoon baking powder
¼ teaspoon salt
½ cup milk
¾ cup sugar
1 tablespoon cornstarch
½ pint heavy cream, whipped and
    sweetened

Drain liquid from cherries; add enough water to it to make 1 cup of liquid; heat to boiling. Turn cherries into a greased, 8-inch square baking pan. Cream together the ¾ cup sugar and the butter; stir in the shredded bran. Sift flour again with baking powder and salt. Add dry ingredients to the creamed mixture alternately with the milk. Then spread batter evenly over the cherries.

Mix together the remaining ¾ cup sugar and the cornstarch, and sprinkle evenly over the batter. Pour the hot juice over all. Bake in a moderate oven (350°) for 1 hour, or until the topping is golden brown. Top with sweetened whipped cream. Makes 8 servings.

Arab Pumpkin Pudding

Bake this pumpkin, raisin, and almond combination in an attractive casserole, then serve it from the baking container.

1 can (1 lb.) pumpkin
1 cup sugar
½ cup sliced almonds or chopped
    filberts
2 tablespoons raisins
2 tablespoons butter
2 tablespoons flour
1½ cups milk
1 teaspoon cinnamon
¼ teaspoon each salt and vanilla

Combine in a large bowl the pumpkin, ½ cup of the sugar, ¼ cup of the nuts, and 1 tablespoon of the raisins. In a heavy saucepan, melt the butter; stir in the flour, allowing to brown. Add milk and cook slowly until thickened, stirring. Combine the cinnamon, salt, and remaining ½ cup sugar; add to the sauce along with the vanilla. Blend well half of the sauce with the pumpkin mixture; pour into a buttered 1½-quart casserole. Pour remaining sauce over top and sprinkle with remaining nuts and raisins. Bake in a moderate oven (350°) for 40 minutes. Serve warm or chilled. Makes 6 to 8 servings.

Pumpkin Flan
with Caramel Sauce

Garnish this delicately spiced pumpkin flan with a sprinkling of sliced walnuts in the center and a ring of pecan or walnut halves around the edge. Use rum for flaming.

4 eggs
½ cup sugar
½ teaspoon each salt and cinnamon
¼ teaspoon each ground ginger,
    allspice, and nutmeg
1 cup light cream or milk
1 cup canned pumpkin
Caramel Sauce
Pecan or walnut halves
3 tablespoons dark rum (optional)

Beat together the eggs, sugar, salt, cinnamon, ginger, allspice, and nutmeg just until blended. Scald cream; immediately beat into egg mixture. Then beat in the pumpkin until smooth. Pour into a buttered, 8-inch layer cake pan placed in ½ inch hot water; bake in a moderate oven (350°) about 30 minutes or until done. Cool to room temperature; run a knife around edge of pan; turn out on serving plate and chill until time to serve. Pour Caramel Sauce over top, and garnish with the nuts.

To flame, heat rum in a small pan until it begins to steam. Ignite; pour flaming rum over the flan. Cut in wedges to serve. Makes 8 to 10 servings.

Caramel Sauce
½ cup brown sugar, firmly packed
1½ tablespoons each water and butter

In a small saucepan combine brown sugar with water and butter; bring to a boil, stirring until dissolved. Cool and pour over flan. Makes about ½ cup sauce.

Chocolate Soufflé

2 tablespoons butter or margarine
2 tablespoons flour
¾ cup milk
2 tablespoons cocoa
½ cup sugar
3 eggs, separated
1 teaspoon vanilla
¼ teaspoon salt

Melt butter and blend in flour. Add milk gradually, and cook, stirring, until thick and smooth. Stir in cocoa and 2 tablespoons of the sugar. Beat egg yolks into the hot mixture and remove from heat. Add vanilla.

Beat egg whites with salt until soft peaks form; then add remaining sugar gradually, and continue beating until short distinct peaks form. Fold in chocolate sauce in 2 parts, and turn into a generously buttered and sugar-dusted 1½-quart soufflé dish or into 5 individual (about 1 cup capacity) dishes; fit a lightly buttered foil collar around dish (extending about an inch above rim). Bake in a hot oven (400°) for 30 minutes for a large soufflé dish, 20 minutes for individual dishes, or until the soufflé feels set when touched lightly with your finger. Remove collar and serve at once. Makes 5 servings.

Fruit Soufflé

Summer fruits are an invitation to experiment with flavors in this basic soufflé. Peaches, apples, pears, nectarines, to name a few, are all delicious. Dark or red fruits tend to discolor the soufflé.

3 tablespoons each *butter or margarine and flour*
1 cup fruit pulp (whirled smooth in a blender or rubbed through a wire sieve)
Sugar to taste (2 or 3 tablespoons)
Flavoring (see below)
4 or 5 eggs, separated
Sugar (at least ¼ cup)

Fruits suitable for soufflés

Fresh, canned, or frozen peaches, apricots, or nectarines; flavor with ½ teaspoon almond extract
Fresh apples, cooked, or canned applesauce; flavor with ¾ teaspoon vanilla or ¼ teaspoon grated orange peel
Fresh pineapple, or canned crushed pineapple
Fresh or canned grapefruit
Fresh oranges or canned mandarins; flavor with ½ teaspoon grated orange peel

In a saucepan melt butter and stir in flour. Sweeten pulp slightly (use about 2 or 3 tablespoons sugar); blend into butter mixture. Cook, stirring, until thickened. Remove from heat and add flavoring and egg yolks. Whip egg whites until they hold soft peaks; gradually beat in ¼ cup sugar until whites hold short distinct peaks. Fold half the whites thoroughly into sauce; fold in remaining whites as thoroughly as you like. Pour into a buttered and sugar-dusted 1½-quart soufflé dish; fit a lightly buttered foil collar around dish (it should extend about an inch above rim). Bake in a moderately hot oven (375°) for 15 minutes, then remove collar gently and sprinkle top with more sugar if you like. (Do not remove from oven.) Continue baking 15 minutes longer. Makes 4 or 5 servings.

Steamed Chocolate Pudding

A hard sauce, with whipped cream folded in, is a nice complement to this bittersweet chocolate flavored pudding.

3 tablespoons butter or margarine
⅔ cup sugar
1 egg
2½ squares (2½ oz.) unsweetened chocolate
2¼ cups all-purpose flour (sift before measuring)
3 teaspoons baking powder
½ teaspoon salt
1 cup milk
1 teaspoon vanilla

Cream butter and sugar together until fluffy; add egg and beat until light. Melt chocolate over hot, not boiling, water; add to creamed mixture and beat well. Sift flour again with baking powder and salt. Add dry ingredients to creamed mixture alternately with the milk, beating after each addition. Stir in vanilla. Spoon mixture into a greased 1½-quart mold; cover; steam for 2 hours.

Whipped Hard Sauce

4 tablespoons (¼ cup) butter or margarine
1 cup powdered sugar
½ teaspoon vanilla
¼ cup heavy cream, whipped

To make the sauce, cream the 4 tablespoons butter with the powdered sugar and vanilla. Whip cream until thick; fold into the creamed mixture. Serve sauce over slices of hot pudding. Makes 8 servings.

Spicy Dark Steamed Pudding

Moist, rich steamed pudding adds a sweet, old-fashioned ending to any meal.

1 cup persimmon purée (whirl about 3
    ripe, seeded, and peeled persimmons
    in a blender) or 1 cup applesauce
2 teaspoons soda
½ cup butter or margarine, at room
    temperature
1 cup sugar
2 eggs
2 tablespoons water
1 teaspoon each vanilla and lemon juice
1 cup all-purpose flour (sift before
    measuring)
1 teaspoon ground cinnamon
¼ teaspoon each salt and ground
    allspice
½ cup chopped nuts
1 cup raisins or chopped dates

Blend purée with soda. Beat butter and sugar together until creamy; add eggs, water, vanilla, and lemon juice, beating until blended.

Sift flour again with cinnamon, salt, and allspice; gradually stir into creamy mixture with purée, nuts, and raisins.

Pour batter into a 6-cup greased metal mold; cover with foil. Set an inch-high trivet or ring from a cake pan with removable bottom in a large kettle; set a rack on top. Pour in ¾ inch water and set mold on rack. Cover kettle and cook 2½ hours over gently boiling water, adding hot water as needed.

Invert pudding onto a platter. Serve with Lemon Sauce. Makes 8 to 10 servings.

Lemon Sauce

1 cup sugar
½ cup butter or margarine, at room
    temperature
¼ cup lemon juice
1 egg
1 teaspoon grated lemon peel

In a small pan, prepare a syrup by combining sugar, butter and lemon juice; cook, stirring, over medium heat until mixture boils. Beat egg with lemon peel and 3 tablespoons water. Beat ¼ cup hot syrup into egg mixture; then stir egg mixture into remaining syrup; cook for 1 minute until thickened. Serve hot.

Crème Brûlée

Crème brûlée (burnt cream) is an elegant dessert that is particularly suitable for a small dinner party. With its delightful contrast of smooth, rich custard and crunchy, caramelized sugar topping, it is almost certain to delight guests. Unlike the traditional French recipe, this version is studded with chopped toasted almonds.

1 pint (2 cups) heavy cream
1-inch piece vanilla bean or 1 teaspoon
    vanilla
6 egg yolks
¼ cup granulated sugar
⅛ teaspoon salt
2 tablespoons brandy, rum, or
    orange-flavored liqueur (optional)
½ cup finely chopped toasted
    blanched almonds
About ¾ cup light brown sugar

Heat cream with the vanilla bean (if used) over low heat until scalded. Beat egg yolks with the granulated sugar and salt until thoroughly blended. Gradually stir the hot cream into the egg yolk mixture, discarding the vanilla bean. Turn into the top of the double boiler and place over hot water (just under the boiling point). Stirring constantly, cook until the mixture coats the spoon in a thick opaque layer. Remove from heat and place in a pan of cold water to cool quickly. Stir in brandy, if desired, the vanilla (if vanilla bean was not used), and the toasted almonds. Pour into a 9-inch pie dish or baking dish and chill, uncovered.

At serving time (or not more than 4 hours earlier), sift the brown sugar over the top, using a coarse-textured flour sifter or pressing sugar though a sieve with the back of the spoon. Make an even layer of sugar ¼-inch thick. (It's important that no custard shows through the sugar layer, as it may become watery under the broiler.) Set the baking dish in an oven-proof dish of crushed ice and place about 6 inches under a preheated broiler, just until sugar caramelizes. (This takes only a few seconds.) Serve immediately or refrigerate until serving time.

To serve, break through crust with a spoon, keeping as much of the crust on top of each serving of custard as possible. Serve plain or accompany with fresh strawberries, raspberries, or sliced peaches, sweetened to taste; or with fresh pear halves, poached in syrup and then chilled. Makes 6 servings.

Pots de Crème

3 cups heavy cream
9 egg yolks
⅓ cup sugar
Dash salt
2 teaspoons vanilla

Scald cream. Beat egg yolks with sugar, salt, and vanilla until mixed but not thick. Add scalded cream and mix well. Put 12 little "pots" (or Chinese tea-cups, or small custard cups) in a shallow 1 to 1½-quart baking dish and add 1 inch hot water. Divide the cream mixture among the pots and bake in a moderately slow oven (325°) for 15 minutes, or until a silver knife comes out clean. (These can be made the day before and refrigerated overnight, if you wish.) Serve cold but not chilled. Makes 12 servings.

Strawberries with Russian Cream

Snowy white and smooth as velvet, this creamy spread is served with fresh strawberries and wafer cookies.

¾ cup sugar
1 envelope unflavored gelatin
½ cup water
1 cup whipping cream or half-and-half
   (light cream)
1½ cups sour cream
1 teaspoon vanilla
Strawberries
Crisp vanilla or lemon-flavored cookies

In a small pan, blend together sugar and unflavored gelatin. Add water and mix well; let stand about 5 minutes, then bring to full boil, stirring constantly. Remove sugar mixture from heat; add whipping cream. In a bowl, mix sour cream with vanilla, then gradually, and smoothly beat in hot sugar mixture.

Pour mixture into a pretty serving bowl (4 or 5-cup size). To make individual desserts, pour cream equally into 8 small serving dishes (about ½ cup size). Cover and chill until set, at least 4 hours.

Accompany cream with strawberries and cookies. Eat with a spoon, or mound cream onto cookies and top each bite with a fresh berry. Makes 8 servings.

Fresh Pear Pudding

2 eggs
1 cup sugar
⅔ cup all-purpose flour (sift before
   measuring)
¼ teaspoon salt
2½ teaspoons baking powder
1 cup chopped peeled and cored fresh
   pears
1 cup chopped walnuts
2 teaspoons lemon juice
½ cup flaked coconut
Whipped cream

Beat the eggs thoroughly. Gradually beat in sugar, beating until fluffy. Sift flour again with salt and baking powder into the egg mixture. Blend well. Fold in the pears, nut meats, and lemon juice. Pour into a buttered baking dish (9 inches square). Sprinkle the flaked coconut over top. Bake in a moderate oven (350°) for 30 minutes. Serve warm or cold, cut in squares and topped with whipped cream. Makes 6 to 8 servings.

Coffee Custard Supreme

3½ cups light cream or milk
1½ teaspoons instant coffee powder
½ teaspoon cinnamon
5 eggs
⅔ cup sugar
½ teaspoon salt
2 teaspoons vanilla
Butterscotch or chocolate sauce, or
   sweetened whipped cream

Heat cream, coffee powder, and cinnamon to scalding. Combine with eggs beaten with sugar, salt, and vanilla. Pour into a shallow 1½-quart baking dish (or dish in which the custard is 1¼ to 1½ inches deep). Place in a pan of hot water half the depth of the custard. Bake in a moderate oven (350°) until a knife, inserted in center, comes out clean (35 to 40 minutes). Cool. Serve plain, or with sauce or whipped cream. Makes 6 servings.

Rum Pudding with Raspberry Sauce

This snowy white molded dessert has raspberry sauce spooned over the top.

1 envelope (1 tablespoon) unflavored
  gelatin
¼ cup cold water
5 egg yolks
¾ cup sugar
2 cups milk, scalded
½ cup light rum (or use rum flavoring
  to taste with additional ½ cup milk)
Dash salt
1 cup (½ pint) heavy cream, whipped

Soak gelatin in cold water. Beat the egg yolks with sugar until thick and lemon colored. Slowly stir in the hot milk. Pour into the top of a double boiler and cook over hot (not boiling) water, stirring constantly, until thick and smooth. Stir in gelatin until dissolved; cool. Fold in rum, whipped cream; turn into 1½-quart mold. Chill until set. Makes 6 to 8 servings.

Raspberry Sauce

1 cup raspberry purée from canned or
  frozen raspberries
¾ cup red currant jelly
1 tablespoon cornstarch

To make the sauce, press canned or frozen raspberries with their juice through a fine sieve to make 1 cup. Heat ¾ cup of the purée; stir in jelly. Blend cornstarch with the remaining ¼ cup purée, stir into the hot mixture and cook until thickened and clear; cool. Makes 6 to 8 servings.

Pine Nut Pudding

This traditional Middle Eastern dessert is a sweet farina pudding with the crunch and delicate flavor of pine nuts.

½ cup (¼ pound) butter or margarine
1 cup farina
½ cup coarsely chopped pine nuts
2 cups water
1 cup sugar
Light or heavy cream (optional)

Melt butter in a large frying pan; add farina and ¼ cup of the pine nuts. Cook over medium heat, stirring constantly, until golden brown. In a saucepan combine water and sugar; boil rapidly for 5 minutes. Remove from heat and gradually stir the farina-pine-nut mixture into the syrup. Simmer over low heat, stirring occasionally, for 15 minutes. Turn into a serving bowl and sprinkle remaining pine nuts over the pudding. Serve plain or with cream to pour over top. Makes 6 to 8 servings.

Orange-Date Sponge Pudding

As this pudding bakes, a tender cake rises to the top and a richly blended sauce of orange and dates forms beneath. Spoon sauce over the warm cake to serve.

1½ tablespoons butter or margarine
1 cup sugar
2 eggs, separated
Grated peel and juice of 1
  medium-sized orange
2 tablespoons flour
1 cup milk
1 cup chopped pitted dates

Cream together butter and sugar; add egg yolks, orange peel, and orange juice and blend thoroughly. Mix in flour, milk, and chopped dates. Beat egg whites until they hold stiff peaks (do not overbeat) and fold into butter and sugar mixture. Pour batter into a greased and flour-dusted, 9-inch square baking pan. Set in a pan of hot water and bake in a moderate oven (350°) for 50 minutes. Spoon into serving dishes and serve warm. Makes 6 to 8 servings.

Frozen and Refrigerator Desserts

Imposing as they may appear, most of these desserts are not difficult to make, and many can be made hours or even days before you want to serve them. Some molded and frozen mousses, colorful parfaits, elaborate trifles, and refrigerator-mellowed cake and pie creations are undeniably rich, and a small serving will suffice to top off a dinner; but they are good enough to make almost anyone ignore calories, at least temporarily. On the lighter side are extra-smooth, delightfully flavored hand-cranked ice creams and some made in automatic freezers, fruit sherbets and ices, and creamy puddings that develop character by chilling. All are delicious alone, or accompanied by crisp cookies.

Fresh Mint Sherbet

Crushed mint leaves flavor this exceptionally cool and smooth-tasting sherbet.

¾ cup sugar
1 cup water
1 cup fresh mint sprigs
½ cup lemon juice
Few drops green food coloring
2 egg whites
¼ cup sugar

Combine the ¾ cup sugar and water; boil until sugar dissolves. In a large heat-proof bowl, crush mint with a pastry blender or wooden spoon. Pour the boiling syrup over the mint; crush leaves again. Cover, and allow to stand until cool. Stir in lemon juice and food coloring. Strain and discard mint. Pour syrup into freezer tray (about 1 quart) and freeze until mushy. Beat egg whites until foamy, add ¼ cup sugar a tablespoon at a time, and beat until egg whites are stiff and sugar is dissolved. Remove mint ice from freezer, turn into a chilled bowl, and beat until smooth. Fold in beaten egg whites, blending until mixture is smooth. Return to freezer tray, and freeze until firm. Makes about 8 servings.

Ginger Sherbet

This is easy to make and very refreshing.

1 quart lemon sherbet
⅓ to ½ cup finely chopped candied
*   ginger*

Let lemon sherbet soften slightly. Mix in the chopped ginger. Refreeze. Serve plain or with fruit.

Garnish coffee-flavored Norwegian fromage (recipe, page 60) with whipped cream and your favorite fresh fruit.

Pineapple Sherbet

To mellow the flavor, this sherbet should be made at least the day before you want to serve it. Let stand in the refrigerator for 20 to 30 minutes to soften slightly before serving.

2 eggs, separated
¾ cup sugar
1 can (9 oz.) crushed pineapple
2 tablespoons lemon juice
2 cups commercial buttermilk
1 teaspoon (part of a package)
   unflavored gelatin
1 tablespoon water

Combine the egg yolks, ½ cup of the sugar, the pineapple (including the syrup), lemon juice, and buttermilk in the blender; whirl until blended (or beat together with rotary beater). Soften the gelatin in water; stir over hot water until dissolved; then blend into buttermilk mixture. Pour into a 2-quart container and freeze until firm around the outer edges of the container, about 1½ hours.

Beat the egg whites until soft, moist peaks form; gradually beat in the remaining ¼ cup sugar and continue beating until egg whites hold firm peaks. Break the partially frozen sherbet into chunks, pour it into a chilled bowl and beat until fluffy, then fold into egg white mixture. Return to freezer container and freeze until it is firm. Makes about 1½ quarts.

Papaya Sherbet

This is simply papaya pulp blended with lemon juice. It's intriguing in flavor but won't have pleasing smooth texture unless you make it in an ice cream freezer, turned by hand or electrically. (See recipe for Vanilla Ice Cream for freezing directions.)

3 very large or 4 medium-sized fully
   ripe papayas
¼ cup lemon juice
2 cups sugar

Peel papaya and scrape out seeds, then force pulp through a wire strainer or whirl it in a blender. Add lemon juice and sugar. Freeze until firm.

Fresh Orange Sherbet

Garnish servings of this sherbet with fresh orange slices or drained canned mandarins and mint sprigs.

2 cups milk
1 cup sugar
Juice of 2 large oranges
Juice of 1 lemon

Combine milk, sugar, orange juice, and lemon juice. Pour into a freezer tray; freeze until mushy. Pour into a bowl and beat with a rotary mixer until creamy. Return to freezer until firm. Makes about 3 cups, or 6 servings.

Vanilla Ice Cream

This crank freezer vanilla ice cream is the basic recipe for the flavored ice creams that follow.

3-inch piece of vanilla bean pod or
   1½ teaspoons vanilla
1½ cups milk
1 tablespoon cornstarch
¼ teaspoon salt
¾ cup sugar
4 egg yolks
1½ cups heavy cream

Split vanilla pod and scrape seeds into milk; drop in the pod. Scald. Combine cornstarch, salt, sugar, and slightly beaten egg yolks, and mix well. Beat in a little of the scalded milk, then combine the two mixtures and cook over a low heat or in a double boiler, stirring constantly, until thick and smooth. (Add vanilla if vanilla bean was not used.) Chill, then stir in cream.

Pour into freezer can, not more than two-thirds full, and chill thoroughly (in your food freezer if there is room, or in the refrigerator). Assemble. Freeze, using 1 part ice cream salt (rock salt) to 8 parts crushed ice. Turn until crank is hard to move, about 15 minutes for 2-quart size. Drain off ice water, carefully remove lid of freezer container, lift out dasher. Serve at once; or pack ice cream into can, cover can with waxed paper or foil and replace top, add ice and salt (1 part salt to 4 parts ice) until can is covered, then cover with newspapers or burlap and let stand for an hour or two. Makes 1 generous quart.

Chocolate Flake Ice Cream

Follow recipe for Vanilla Ice Cream, with these changes: Reduce sugar to ½ cup. Add 1 cup shaved sweet or semi-sweet chocolate (use a potato peeler, or grate on shredder side of grater). Makes 1¼ quarts.

Praline Ice Cream

Follow recipe for Vanilla Ice Cream, with these changes: Reduce sugar to ¼ cup and add 1 cup coarsely crushed pralines (below). Makes 1¼ quarts.

Praline: In a heavy skillet, put ½ cup *each* shelled unblanched filberts and almonds. Add 1 cup granulated sugar and cook over medium heat until the sugar melts and the skins on the nuts split. Do not stir, but tilt the pan until the sugar is completely melted and a golden brown. Pour into a buttered pan and spread thin. Let harden, then put in a heavy paper or cloth bag and crush with a mallet.

Sherry Macaroon Ice Cream

Follow recipe for Vanilla Ice Cream, with these changes: Use ¼ cup dry sherry in place of ¼ cup milk. Omit vanilla. Just before freezing add 1 cup almond macaroon crumbs about the size of small peas. Makes 1¼ quarts.

Peach Sorbet

Sorbet is another name for an ice made with the juice of several fruits and the pulp of one of them (in this case, peaches). This one is tart and good for a light dessert.

¾ cup fresh peach pulp (sieved or
   whirled in a blender)
¼ cup sugar
¾ cup orange juice
2 tablespons lemon juice

Combine peach pulp with sugar, orange juice, and lemon juice. Pour into a 1-quart freezer tray and freeze until mushy, stirring occasionally. Turn into a bowl and beat until smooth with an electric or rotary mixer. Return to tray and freeze until firm, stirring once or twice. Makes about 1 pint.

Frozen Fruit Pudding

The fruits in this dessert are particularly colorful against the white base.

¼ cup seedless raisins
¼ cup candied cherries, finely chopped
¼ cup chopped nuts
¼ cup drained crushed pineapple
½ cup sugar
¼ cup pineapple syrup
2 egg whites
Pinch of salt
1 tablespoon lemon juice
1 cup (½ pint) heavy cream, whipped

Cover raisins with cold water, bring to a boil, and simmer 5 minutes; drain. Combine drained raisins, cherries, nuts, and pineapple. Boil sugar and pineapple syrup together until thick, about 5 minutes. Beat egg whites with salt until stiff; pour hot pineapple syrup over egg whites, beating constantly. Add fruits, nuts, and lemon juice. Blend whipped cream into egg white mixture. Pour into a 5 by 9-inch loaf pan. Freeze for 24 hours. Makes 8 servings.

Frozen Fruit Yogurts

Here's a creamy dessert with the consistency of home-made ice cream but only half the calories and a fraction of the store-bought cost. You can make the yogurt mixture early in the day and store it in the refrigerator until you're ready to turn it in the ice cream freezer. Or take it along on a picnic in an ice chest and turn it at the site.

Sweetened Fruit Mixture (suggestions
  follow)
3 eggs, separated
¼ teaspoon each salt and cream of
  tartar
¼ cup sugar
2 quarts homemade or purchased
  unflavored yogurt

In a 3-quart pan, combine fruit and sugar (plus honey, if used) for fruit mixture of your choice (suggestions follow). Bring to a boil, stirring, over high heat. Reduce heat to medium, and cook, stirring constantly, until fruit softens and partially disintegrates (1 to 4 minutes). Remove from heat; stir in fruit juices, spices, and flavorings.

In a small bowl, lightly beat egg yolks; stir in about ½ cup of the hot fruit mixture. Then stir yolk mixture into fruit mixture; cool to room temperature.

In a large mixing bowl, beat egg whites until frothy; add salt and cream of tartar beating until soft peaks form. Gradually add ¼ cup sugar and continue beating until stiff peaks form.

Turn yogurt into a 5-quart or larger bowl; fold fruit mixture into yogurt until well blended. Then gently fold yogurt-fruit mixture into egg whites. At this point, you can cover and refrigerate several hours. When ready to process, transfer to a gallon-size or larger, hand-crank or electric ice cream freezer.

Assemble freezer according to manufacturer's directions, using about 4 parts ice to 1 part rock salt. When hand-cranking becomes difficult or electric motor stalls, remove the dasher. Once the yogurt has been turned and frozen, you can tuck the metal container in the freezer compartment of your refrigerator until serving time. Away from home, repack the container in ice and salt to keep it soft-frozen for 3 hours. Makes 1 gallon.

Sweetened Fruit Mixtures

Apricot-orange. Use 4 cups thinly sliced unpeeled ripe apricots, 2 cups sugar, 2 tablespoons lemon juice, ½ cup orange juice, 1 teaspoon grated orange peel, and 4 teaspoons vanilla.

Banana-honey. Measure 4 cups thinly sliced ripe bananas, then coarsely mash them. Also use 1¼ cups sugar, ¾ cup honey, 3 tablespoons lemon juice, and 2 tablespoons vanilla.

Blackberry. Use 4 cups lightly packed whole fresh (or unsweetened frozen, defrosted) blackberries, 2 cups sugar, and 4 teaspoons *each* lemon juice and vanilla.

Blueberry. Use 4 cups whole fresh (or unsweetened frozen, defrosted) blueberries, 1¾ cups sugar, 2 tablespoons lemon juice, and 1 tablespoon vanilla.

Papaya. Coarsely mash enough peeled and seeded fruit (2 to 3 papayas) to make 2½ cups purée. Also use 2 cups sugar, 2 teaspoons vanilla, and ¼ cup lime juice.

Peach. Use 4 cups sliced peeled peaches, 2 cups firmly packed brown sugar, 3 tablespoons vanilla, and ¾ teaspoon *each* ground nutmeg and cinnamon.

Raspberry. Use 4 cups lightly packed fresh (or unsweetened frozen, defrosted) raspberries, 2 cups sugar, and 4 teaspoons *each* lemon juice and vanilla.

Yogurt Cheese Pie

Bake this rich-tasting dessert ahead, so you can serve it well chilled.

1¾ cups graham cracker crumbs
¾ cup sugar
⅓ cup melted butter or margarine
1 large package (8 oz.) cream cheese,
  at room temperature
3 eggs
2 teaspoons vanilla
¼ teaspoon salt
2 cups unflavored yogurt
2 cups fresh rapsberries or sliced
  nectarines, sweetened to taste

Combine crumbs, ¼ cup of the sugar, and butter. Press mixture over bottom and sides of a 10-inch metal or glass pie pan. Bake in a 350° oven for 5 minutes; let cool.

In a mixing bowl, combine cream cheese with remaining ½ cup sugar. Beat in eggs, one at a time, then add vanilla and salt; beat at medium speed until light and well creamed. Using low speed, blend in yogurt. Pour into crumb-lined pan and bake in a 350° oven for 40 minutes, or until dry when lightly touched.

Cool, then chill at least 4 hours or as long as overnight. To serve, cut in wedges and spoon sweetened fruit with their juices over each serving. Makes 8 servings.

Frozen Strawberry Mold

Thin, crisp sugar cookies are good with this molded fruit dessert.

1 quart strawberries
¼ cup sugar
2 teaspoons lemon juice
2 cups (1 pint) heavy cream
½ cup powdered sugar
Few grains salt

Wash and hull berries, saving a few whole ones for garnish. Mash remainder with sugar and lemon juice. Put through sieve or food mill, or purée in electric blender. Whip cream; sweeten with powdered sugar and add salt. Fold in puréed berries and pour into 1½-quart mold. Cover with foil. Freeze until firm; unmold and garnish with whole berries. Makes 6 servings.

Apricot-Banana Mousse

Its tart base is a blend of fresh apricots and bananas; the topping is fruit-flavored whipped cream flecked with walnuts.

1 quart sweetened, cooked fresh apricot
halves or 2 large cans (1 lb. 13 oz.)
each apricots, drained
2 large bananas
1 cup granulated sugar
1 cup water
Juice of 1 lemon
1 pint heavy cream
2 tablespoons powdered sugar
1 cup very finely chopped walnuts

Put apricots through a sieve; purée bananas and add to the apricots. In a saucepan combine granulated sugar and the water, and boil until a thick syrup is formed. Stir sugar syrup and lemon juice into the fruit mixture; cool. When apricot-banana mixture is cold, whip cream and fold in powdered sugar and nuts. Then fold 1¾ cups of the apricot mixture into the whipped cream. Pour the remaining apricot-banana mixture into a fancy 2½-quart mold and spoon over the fruit-flavored whipped cream. Cover with foil and freeze without stirring for 4 hours or until firm. To serve, dip mold in warm water and invert on a platter. Makes 8 servings.

Peanut Brittle Mousse

This dessert is so simple a ten-year-old can make it.

½ pound peanut brittle
2 cups heavy cream
Coarsely chopped peanut brittle or
peanuts

Put ½ pound peanut brittle through the food chopper, using a coarse blade. Whip cream. Combine the two mixtures quickly and pour into an ice cube tray. Freeze until firm. Serve it topped with a garnish of coarsely chopped peanut brittle or peanuts. Makes about 1 quart.

Frozen Peaches and Cream

Here are fresh golden peaches made glamorous with a crushed wafer crust, frothy whipped cream. This dish is impressive, but easy to make.

1½ cups crushed vanilla wafer crumbs
¼ cup melted butter
2 tablespoons orange juice
1 tablespoon lemon juice
½ pound marshmallows
1 cup crushed fresh peaches, drained
1 cup heavy cream, whipped
Peach slices for garnish

Combine the vanilla wafer crumbs with melted butter and pat evenly over sides and bottom of a refrigerator tray or an 8-inch cake pan. Set in the refrigerator while making the filling. Heat orange and lemon juice to the boiling point. Add the marshmallows, reduce heat, and stir until marshmallows are dissolved. Cool slightly. Stir in the drained peaches. Fold in whipped cream. Pour into the wafer crust and freeze for 3 to 4 hours. (Freezing compartment of refrigerator can be left at normal setting.) Makes 6 to 8 servings.

Napoleon Parfait

Whenever you put coffee and chocolate together, you have a flavor treat ahead.

¾ cup sugar
⅓ cup strong coffee
4 egg yolks
1 square (1 oz.) unsweetened chocolate, melted
1 teaspoon vanilla
1½ cups heavy cream
Cinnamon

Cook sugar and coffee together for 5 minutes. Beat egg yolks until light, then slowly pour over them the hot coffee syrup, mixing thoroughly. Stir in melted chocolate. When cool, add vanilla and fold into cream that has been beaten until it just begins to hold its shape. Turn into refrigerator tray and freeze without stirring. Spoon into parfait glasses and sprinkle a bit of cinnamon over each serving. Makes 6 servings.

Chocolate-Coffee Freezer Torte

This quick-and-easy dessert never fails to get compliments — a great choice when something spectacular is called for.

1 cup crushed coconut-macaroon cooky crumbs
2 tablespoons melted butter or margarine
1 pint chocolate ice cream, slightly softened
½ cup chocolate-flavored syrup
1 pint coffee ice cream, slightly softened
About 4 ounces chocolate-covered, hard toffee candy bars, coarsely chopped

Stir together cooky crumbs and butter. Lightly press into bottom of a 9-inch cake pan with a removable bottom. Bake in a 350° oven for 8 to 10 minutes or until lightly browned. Cool.

Spread chocolate ice cream in an even layer over cooled crust; drizzle evenly with ¼ cup of the syrup and freeze until firm. Then top with an even layer of coffee ice cream, sprinkle evenly with crushed candy and drizzle remaining syrup over top. Cover and freeze until firm. Makes 6 to 8 servings.

Raspberry Macaroon Parfait

This parfait, with its layers of red raspberries, cream, and sherried cookies, looks like a party dessert. You'll find it extremely simple to assemble.

3 dozen macaroons
½ cup dry sherry
2 cups sugared raspberries
½ pint (1 cup) heavy cream, whipped
½ cup blanched almonds, chopped and toasted

Soak macaroons in sherry, then crumble. In individual parfait glasses, alternate the crumbled macaroons, berries, whipped cream, and chopped nuts, ending with a topping of whipped cream, nuts, and a few whole berries. Chill. Makes 4 to 6 servings.

Blueberry Lemon Custard Trifle

With blueberry jam, ladyfingers, white port wine, lemon custard sauce, and a slivered almond topping, this trifle is a delightful blend of flavors.

2 dozen large ladyfingers
1 cup blueberry jam
6 tablespoons white port or muscatel
   wine
Lemon Custard
½ pint (1 cup) heavy cream
Powdered sugar
Almond extract
½ cup slivered almonds

Split ladyfingers, spread with jam, and put back together, sandwich-fashion. Arrange about half of them in the bottom of a 9-inch square baking pan or in a bowl, all running the same direction. Sprinkle with 3 tablespoons of the wine. Arrange remaining ladyfingers in a row running the opposite direction. Sprinkle with remaining wine. Pour over the cooled lemon custard. Chill at least 4 hours. At serving time, whip cream until stiff, sweeten and flavor with powdered sugar and a few drops of almond extract. Drop in puffs on top of ladyfingers and custard. Sprinkle with slivered almonds. Makes 12 servings.

Lemon Custard

½ cup sugar
2 tablespoons cornstarch
¼ teaspoon salt
1½ cups hot water
2 eggs
1 tablespoon butter
½ teaspoon grated lemon peel
¼ cup lemon juice

Combine sugar, cornstarch, and salt in the top of double boiler. Add hot water. Place over direct heat and bring to a boil, stirring constantly. Boil until clear, about 1 minute. Beat eggs in a large bowl. Gradually add hot cornstarch mixture, stirring rapidly. Return to top of double boiler and place over boiling water. Cook for 3 minutes, stirring constantly. Remove from heat; stir in butter, lemon peel, and lemon juice. Cool.

Fromage Glacé

For a refreshing summer dessert, serve this flavorful cheese mold surrounded by thin crescents of icy honeydew and cantaloupe balls, accented with a few fresh berries.

2 envelopes (2 tablespoons) unflavored
   gelatin
½ cup cold water
½ cup (¼ pound) softened butter
4 egg yolks
8 ounces Camembert cheese
4 ounces Liederkranz cheese
2 ounces blue cheese
1 cup heavy cream, whipped
Garnishes

Soften gelatin in water; place over hot water until gelatin dissolves to liquid. Beat soft butter until creamy; set aside. With electric beater, beat egg yolks in large mixing bowl until thick and lemon colored. Remove crusts from Camembert, Liederkranz, and blue cheeses. Break cheeses into bits and drop into egg yolks; beat until mixture is blended smoothly. Add creamed butter and dissolved gelatin; beat until blended. Fold in whipped cream. Turn mixture into a lightly oiled mold (about 5-cup size). Chill until set. At serving time, dip mold in warm water to loosen: turn out on serving platter. Garnish as desired. Makes 12 servings.

Coffee Fromage

This is another Norwegian fromage. Serve it with your choice of fresh fruit and whipped cream. Mandarin oranges are used here, but you may prefer sliced bananas, fresh strawberries, or sliced peaches.

1 envelope (1 tablespoon) unflavored
   gelatin
3 tablespoons water
3 eggs
¾ cup sugar
2 tablespoons instant coffee powder
1 cup heavy cream
Mandarin orange sections for garnish
Whipped cream for garnish

Soften gelatin in water; stir over hot water until dissolved. In large bowl of your electric mixer, beat eggs until frothy, then beat in sugar and instant coffee powder, and continue to beat at medium to high speed for 5 minutes or until very thick.

In small bowl of your electric mixer, whip the cream until almost stiff, then beat in dissolved gelatin. Fold whipped cream into beaten eggs, or beat at lowest speed of mixer until well combined. Turn into a 4 to 5-cup dessert mold and chill 4 to 8 hours. Unmold, garnish with mandarin oranges and whipped cream. Makes 6 servings.

Orange Fromage

In Norway, "fromage" describes a rich, whipped, molded dessert somewhat like a Bavarian cream. You can vary this fromage to make it either lemon or pineapple-flavored instead of orange. Decorate and serve any of the three with fresh fruit or berries and whipped cream.

1 envelope (1 tablespoon) unflavored
   gelatin
¼ cup orange juice
3 eggs
¾ cup sugar
1 tablespoon grated orange peel
1 cup heavy cream
Strawberries, for garnish
Whipped cream, for garnish

Soften gelatin in orange juice; set over hot water and stir until dissolved. In large bowl of your electric mixer, beat eggs until frothy, then beat in sugar and continue to beat at medium to high speed for about 5 minutes, or until very thick. Mix in the grated orange peel.

In small bowl of your electric mixer, whip the cream until almost stiff, then beat in the dissolved gelatin. Fold whipped cream into beaten eggs, or beat at lowest speed until well combined. Turn into a 4 to 5-cup dessert mold and chill 4 to 8 hours or overnight. Unmold, and garnish with strawberries and whipped cream. Makes 6 servings.

Lemon Fromage: Follow recipe for Orange Fromage, using ¼ cup lemon juice in place of orange juice, and 1 tablespoon grated lemon peel in place of orange peel.

Mocha Alaska Pie

Chocolate and coffee flavors blend together deliciously in this frozen dessert that is so easy to prepare ahead.

1 cup chocolate wafer cooky crumbs,
   finely crushed
¼ cup melted butter or margarine
1 tablespoon sugar
1 quart coffee ice cream, softened
1 can (5½ oz.) chocolate sauce
½ cup chopped nuts
3 egg whites
½ teaspoon vanilla
¼ teaspoon cream of tartar
6 tablespoons sugar

In a 9-inch pie pan, mix cooky crumbs, butter, and 1 tablespoon sugar; press evenly over bottom and up sides of pan. Bake in a 350° oven for 10 minutes; let cool.

Spread ice cream in crust and freeze until firm. Drizzle chocolate sauce evenly over ice cream. Sprinkle with nuts; freeze until firm.

Beat together egg whites, vanilla, and cream of tartar until soft peaks form. Add sugar, 1 tablespoon at a time, until stiff peaks form. Swirl meringue evenly over pie, sealing to edge of crust, and return pie to freezer. When ready to serve, place frozen pie in a 450° oven for about 4 minutes, or until meringue is golden. Makes 6 to 8 servings.

Pineapple Baked Alaska with Raspberry and Apricot Sauces

This spectacular dessert is quite easy to assemble. You fill decorative pineapple half shells with ice cream, pineapple chunks, and meringue, and quickly brown the meringue just before serving. Accompany with a choice of homemade fruit sauces or bottled berry syrups.

Lemon Custard Angel Pie

You fill a meringue shell with alternate layers of whipped cream and lemon custard for this handsome dessert. Bake and freeze the meringue shell ahead of time, if you wish, but remove it from the freezer and put in the filling at least 4 hours before you plan to serve it.

6 egg whites
1 teaspoon baking powder
½ teaspoon salt
1½ cups sugar
2 teaspoons each water, vinegar, and
*   vanilla*
¾ cup sugar
7 tablespoons cornstarch
2½ cups milk
6 egg yolks
½ cup lemon juice
2½ teaspoons grated lemon peel
½ pint heavy cream

For the torte, beat egg whites with baking powder and ¼ teaspoon of the salt until stiff. Gradually beat in sugar, alternately with water, vinegar, and vanilla; continue beating until glossy. Spread on bottom and sides of a buttered 10-inch spring-form pan or cheesecake pan with removable bottom. Bake in a slow oven (275°) for 1 hour 20 minutes. (Don't be concerned if cracks appear.) Cool in the pan.

For the filling, combine the ¾ cup sugar, cornstarch, and remaining ¼ teaspoon salt; stir in the milk. Cook, stirring, until thickened. Beat egg yolks until light; blend in milk mixture. Cook, stirring, until thick. Remove from heat and stir in lemon juice and peel. Chill.

About 4 hours (or as long as a day) before serving, whip cream until stiff and spread alternate layers of cold lemon filling and cream in torte; start and end with lemon filling. Chill. Makes 12 servings.

1 large ripe pineapple
1 pint toasted almond ice cream
1 pint pistachio ice cream
1 package (10 oz.) frozen
*   raspberries, thawed*
2 teaspoons lemon juice
1½ cups canned apricots and syrup
4 egg whites
⅛ teaspoon salt
⅛ teaspoon cream of tartar
½ cup sugar

Wash pineapple; but do not remove leaves. With a sharp knife, cut pineapple in half lengthwise, leaves and all. Using a grapefruit knife, cut out the pineapple and remove from shell. Dice the fruit, discarding the core. Spoon half the fruit back into the pineapple shells. Spoon toasted almond ice cream into one pineapple half shell, and spoon the pistachio ice cream into the other. (Or use vanilla ice cream for both.) Cover the ice cream with the remaining pineapple chunks. Place in the freezer until ice cream is firm again.

Meanwhile, prepare the sauces. Place raspberries and their syrup in a blender and blend until smooth. Then press through a sieve to remove seeds. Stir in lemon juice. (Or you can substitute bottled raspberry syrup for the frozen raspberries and lemon juice.) Pour into a small pitcher for serving. Turn canned apricots into a blender and purée until smooth; add enough of their syrup to make a sauce consistency.

Now for the meringue. Beat egg whites until foamy; add salt and cream of tartar, and beat until soft peaks form. Gradually beat in ½ cup sugar, beating until stiff. Spread the meringue over the pineapple half shells, covering completely. Place in a very hot oven (450°) for 5 minutes, or until meringue is slightly browned. Serve at once with the raspberry and apricot sauces. Makes 8 servings.

Fruit Desserts

Light yet satisfying, beautiful to look at, and deceptively simple to make, fruit desserts can be dramatized to serve to guests or simplified for family fare. A fresh, perfectly ripened fruit is impressive without embellishment; or it can be presented in colorful combination with other fruits. In this chapter, you'll find recipes for flaming fruit desserts, refreshing compotes, baked fruit desserts to be served warm from the oven, and many quick and easy ways to adorn the goodness of fresh and preserved fruits.

A EUROPEAN CUSTOM

In Europe, fruit is often served for dessert in its natural state. Sometimes it is presented in bowls of cold water, which cools the fruit without chilling out its flavor. Try serving small, not too fragile fruits this way: a crystal bowl of water, iced if you prefer, in which plump juicy unstemmed cherries, or small bunches of grapes, or even whole apricots and plums are floating. Add a blossom or two as well, and your fruit bowl will make a charming centerpiece.

If you prefer individual servings, arrange an assortment of fruits for each person in a small bowl of cold water or in a small leaf-lined basket. Or surround a mound of powdered sugar (pack sugar into a jigger or small mold and tap it out onto the center of the plate) with large unstemmed strawberries,

Tasteful and tasty pear, upside down in wine glass, is garnished with glacéed fruits, preserves, or ginger (recipe, page 70).

peeled or unpeeled figs, fingers of pineapple, or perhaps wedges of peaches or pears. You might like to accompany the fruit with a glass of wine in which it can be dipped before being sugared.

ELEGANT COMPOTES

There are two delicious ways to serve fruit in a compote. One is to use fresh fruits, peeled, pitted, cored, quartered, or cut in pieces as appropriate, lightly sugared if desired, flavored with wine or liqueur, and chilled before serving. A more elegant compote can be made with poached fruits. In this case, the smaller fruits such as cherries, apricots, loquats, figs, and plums are left whole, while the larger ones such as peaches and pears are peeled and halved. Simmer the fruit gently in a simple syrup (¾ cup water to each cup sugar, cooked for 5 minutes) for about 3 minutes if ripe, until tender if greener fruit is used. Remove fruit carefully, reduce syrup until almost the thickness desired (it thickens upon cooling), and flavor with vanilla or liqueur. (If vanilla bean is used instead of extract, a split piece should be added to the syrup before it is cooked.) Whole blanched almonds can be added to this type of fruit compote. It is often served hot or warm.

Hot Caramel Peaches

1 can (about 1 lb. 14 oz.) cling peach
  halves
¼ cup brown sugar
¾ cup commercial sour cream or unflavored
  yogurt
Cinnamon

In a saucepan, slowly heat peach halves in their own syrup. Place each hot peach half in a small dessert dish and top with 2 teaspoons brown sugar and 2 tablespoons sour cream. Sprinkle with cinnamon. Makes 6 servings.

Honeyed Oranges with Almonds

Select large-sized oranges; peel and slice about ½ inch thick. For each serving arrange 3 orange slices on individual dessert plates, spoon over 1 teaspoon clover honey, and garnish with a generous sprinkle of slivered, toasted almonds.

Honey-Baked Apples

Baked apples filled with dried fruits are delicious with honey added to the filling.

6 large cooking apples
½ cup each sliced pitted dates, dried
  figs, dried prunes
¼ cup seedless raisins
½ cup honey
1½ cups boiling water

Wash and core apples; place in a large baking pan. Combine dates, figs, prunes, raisins, and honey until mixed. Fill apple cores with fruit-honey mixture. Pour water in the baking pan and bake in a moderate oven (350°) for 45 minutes, or until tender. Serve warm or cooled. Makes 6 servings.

Sugar-Crusted Baked Apples

Here's a new way to bake apples: without their peel and sprinkled with a sugar mixture that forms a crisp coating as they bake in orange juice. If you wish, pass rich cream to be poured over these apples.

6 large apples
⅓ cup all-purpose flour, unsifted
⅔ cup sugar
¼ teaspoon cinnamon
⅓ cup butter or margarine
½ cup fresh juice or frozen
  orange juice, reconstituted
¼ cup water

Pare the apples and remove the cores, using an apple corer if you have one. Arrange the apples in a buttered baking dish, about 9 by 13 inches. Combine the flour with the sugar and cinnamon; add the butter and work together until the mixture is well blended. Use part of this mixture to fill the cavities; spread the remainder over the top. Combine the orange juice with the water, and pour into the bottom of the baking pan. Bake, uncovered, in a moderate oven (350°) until the apples are tender, about 1 to 1¼ hours, spooning the pan sauces over the apples several times. Serve warm with some of the sauce from the pan spooned over the apples. Makes 6 servings.

Sour Cream Ambrosia

A sour cream dressing embellishes this date ambrosia, balancing the sweetness of dates and oranges with its tartness.

½ cup commercial sour cream
1 tablespoon brown sugar
½ teaspoon grated orange or lemon
   peel
Pinch of salt
4 oranges, peeled and sliced
½ cup pitted fresh dates, halved
¼ to ½ cup flaked coconut

Combine sour cream, brown sugar, orange peel, and salt; chill. In a serving bowl, layer oranges, dates, and coconut; chill. Serve fruits with topping of sour cream mixture. Makes about 6 servings.

Figs Jacques

The tropical flavors of rum, lime, and mint combine deliciously with figs and lemon sherbet.

8 figs, peeled and cut in halves
3 tablespoons rum or 2½ teaspoons
   rum flavoring
3 tablespoons sugar
Juice of 1 lime
Lemon sherbet
Mint leaves

Combine figs, rum, sugar, and lime juice and divide equally among 4 sherbet glasses or dessert cups. Chill. Top each with a scoop of sherbet, garnish with mint leaves, and serve. Makes 4 servings.

Prune and Apricot Compote

Select large-sized prunes and dried apricot halves. Simmer separately until plump and tender, using 2 cups water for each ½ pound fruit. Drain, and place fruit in a compote. Combine juices, and cook them with sugar to taste and a few paper-thin slices of lemon until lemon is tender. Pour over the fruits, chill, and serve from the compote dish.

Baked Stuffed Peaches

This is an easy dessert to bake while you're eating dinner. Serve the stuffed peaches warm. You might offer cream for those who don't count calories.

6 ripe freestone peaches
½ cup sugar
½ pound almond macaroons, crushed
   (about 2 cups crumbs)
4 egg yolks

Peel and halve peaches; scoop out about 1 teaspoon of the center pulp of each half. Mash pulp; mix with sugar, crushed macaroons, and egg yolks. Place halves close together, cut side up, in greased baking dish (about 9 by 13). Spoon macaroon mixture into center of each. Bake in a slow oven (300°) for 30 minutes, or until peaches are tender. Makes 6 servings.

Mandarin Oranges Flambé

1 can (11 oz.) mandarin oranges,
   undrained
1 to 2 tablespoons brown sugar
Dash of cinnamon
1½ ounces (3 tablespoons) Cointreau
   or Grand Marnier

Place mandarin oranges with their syrup in a chafing dish. Add brown sugar and cinnamon, and heat. After the oranges are warmed, add liqueur and light immediately. Makes 2 servings.

Ginger Ale Melon Cup

This refreshing dessert is especially good made with cantaloupe and watermelon balls, but you could use other combinations, such as honeydew and Persian or Crenshaw. You can use 1½ cups white table wine in place of the ginger ale; in that case add the wine before chilling the combinations.

¼ cup sugar
¼ cup lemon juice
1 quart mixed melon balls
1½ cups chilled ginger ale or
*   sparkling apple juice*
Fresh mint sprigs

Combine sugar and lemon juice; stir until sugar dissolves. Pour over melon balls, and chill thoroughly. To serve, spoon fruit and syrup into sherbet glasses, pour ginger ale over each serving, and garnish with mint sprigs. Makes 6 to 8 servings.

Pineapple - Papaya Fruit Bowl

A rainbow mélange of icy cold marinated fruits handsomely presented in pineapple shells is a perfect choice for a summertime dessert or as a main course salad for a ladies' luncheon.

2 cups fresh pineapple chunks or spears
1 cup fresh papaya slices
1 to 2 cups watermelon balls
1 cup drained canned mandarins
1 cup raspberries, boysenberries, or
*   other berries*
¼ cup kirsch or undiluted frozen
*   orange juice concentrate (thawed)*

Combine pineapple, papaya, watermelon, mandarins, and berries. Pour kirsch or orange juice concentrate evenly over the fruit. Chill for about 30 minutes, stirring occasionally. Serve in 2 halves of chilled large pineapple shell. Makes 4 to 6 servings.

Baked Pears

Baked pears make a pleasing dessert, whether served warm or chilled. Allow one whole fresh pear for each serving.

6 medium pears
Chopped pecans
2 cups firmly packed brown sugar
¼ cup water
2 tablespoons butter or margarine
1 tablespoon rum or 1 teaspoon
*   maple flavoring*

Cut pears in half lengthwise, and remove cores. Arrange, cut side up, in a buttered baking dish. Sprinkle with chopped pecans (1 rounded teaspoon for each half). Make a syrup by cooking together the brown sugar, water, and butter or margarine for 3 or 4 minutes. Add rum or maple flavoring to the syrup, pour over the pears, and cover. Bake in a moderate oven (350°) for 30 minutes, or until the pears are tender. Serve with or without cream. Makes 6 servings.

Strawberry Sherry Cream

6 cups fresh strawberries
½ cup powdered sugar
⅓ cup dry sherry
½ pint heavy cream, whipped

Wash and stem strawberries. Reserve about a third of the finest ones, and mash those remaining. Add powdered sugar and sherry. Let stand 3 or 4 hours, then combine with whipped cream. Gently fold this pink mixture into the whole berries. Makes 6 servings.

Caramelized Western Pears

Pears for this simple recipe should be firm. Serve the fruit hot with the rich caramel sauce.

6 medium pears or apples
1 cup sugar
½ cup butter or margarine
1 cup heavy cream

Peel, quarter, and core pears. In a shallow casserole, place quarters of fruit close together and sprinkle evenly with sugar. Dot each quarter with butter or margarine. Bake in a very hot oven (450°) for about 45 minutes or until sugar turns golden brown. Baste fruit several times during cooking with syrup that forms. Remove pears from baking pan, pour in cream, stir well, return fruit, baste with sauce; continue baking 5 minutes more. Place pears in serving dishes, stir syrup to blend, spoon over fruit and serve hot. Makes 6 to 8 servings.

Raspberries with Grapes

Combine whole raspberries and seedless grapes. Fold into sweetened whipped or sour cream, put in sherbet glasses, and sprinkle with macaroon crumbs or chopped nuts.

Figs Romanoff

2 pounds fresh figs
2 tablespoons curaçao or orange juice
1 pint soft vanilla ice cream
1 cup heavy cream, whipped and
    slightly sweetened
Grated sweet chocolate

Peel figs, if desired, and cut in halves; arrange in a shallow bowl and sprinkle with curaçao or orange juice. Chill. In another bowl, mix ice cream with whipped cream. Fold in figs, sprinkle with grated chocolate, and serve at once. Makes 8 servings.

Poached Purple Plums

Spiced and lightly cooked, these plums can be served either warm or chilled.

About 1½ pounds fresh purple
    prune plums
¾ cup sugar
½ teaspoon pumpkin pie spice (or ⅛
    teaspoon each ground cinnamon,
    ginger, cloves, and nutmeg)
2 tablespoons orange juice
4 teaspoons lemon juice
Dash of salt
2 tablespoons each cornstarch
    and water
Sour cream (optional)

Wash plums, cut in half, and discard pits; you should have 3 cups of fruit. Place in a 2-quart pan; add sugar, pumpkin pie spice, orange juice, lemon juice, and salt. Bring to a boil, reduce heat, and simmer, covered, until plums are just tender when pierced (6 to 8 minutes). Combine cornstarch and water; stir into plums; cook, stirring, until bubbly and clear.

Serve warm; or cool, cover, and refrigerate. Offer fruit in their juice with a dollop of sour cream, if desired. To use as a topping, generously spoon plum mixture over vanilla or toasted almond ice cream or orange or lemon sherbet. Makes 4 to 6 servings.

Stuffed Dessert Figs

Stuffed figs in a rose-colored, rum-flavored syrup make an exotic dessert.

2 cups each sugar and water
2 tablespoons lemon juice
6 whole cloves
1 cinnamon stick
12 large firm black figs
¼ cup each fine-grated coconut
    (or finely chopped shredded coconut)
    and finely chopped candied orange
    peel
2 tablespoons chopped raisins
Rum flavoring to taste, or ⅓ cup rum
Sour cream
Brown sugar

In a saucepan, combine sugar, water, lemon juice, cloves, and cinnamon. Bring to a boil and cook for 5 minutes. Add figs and cook them gently until tender, about 10 minutes. Remove figs from syrup and allow to cool.

To make filling, mix together coconut, orange peel, and raisins. Carefully split each fig on one side. Stuff with about 1 teaspoon of the filling; close, and place in a deep bowl or jar. Remove cloves and cinnamon stick from syrup, add rum flavoring, and heat to boiling. Pour over figs, cover, and chill in refrigerator for 2 days. For each serving, place 3 figs in a stemmed glass. Spoon over some of the sauce, and top with a spoonful of sour cream and a sprinkling of brown sugar. Makes 4 servings.

Grapes Cointreau

1½ cups seedless grapes (canned or
    fresh)
½ cup commercial sour cream
1½ tablespoons Cointreau
Praline Lace Crust (page 92)

Combine grapes with sour cream and Cointreau. Spread evenly in a shallow serving dish. Chill about 1 hour. Top with Praline Lace Crust cut to fit dish (or sprinkle with broken bits of lace crust). To serve, break through crust and spoon out fruit. Makes 4 servings.

Grape Crumbly

This baked fruit dessert has a rich crumb topping. You serve it warm, so it will be welcome on a cool autumn day.

1 quart ripe seedless grapes or seeded
    grapes
1 tablespoon lemon juice
¼ teaspoon salt
⅛ teaspoon nutmeg
½ cup all-purpose flour, unsifted
½ cup brown sugar, firmly packed
¼ cup butter or margarine

Wash, drain, and halve the grapes (remove seeds if necessary). Place in a buttered casserole or baking dish (1½-quart size). Sprinkle with lemon juice, salt, and nutmeg. Bake in a moderately hot oven (375°) for 15 minutes. Meanwhile, mix together until crumbly the flour, brown sugar, and butter. Remove casserole from oven, and stir half the crumb mixture into grapes. Sprinkle remaining crumbs over top. Continue baking about 15 minutes longer. Serve warm with whipped or plain cream. Makes about 6 servings.

Stuffed Cantaloupe

Stuffed cantaloupe makes an interesting dessert that can be prepared and served at a patio meal.

3 cantaloupes
1½ cups heavy cream
3 tablespoons powdered sugar
2 teaspoons vanilla
Pitted Bing cherries

Cut cantaloupes in half, discard seeds, and carefully remove the meat with a grapefruit knife. Then cut it into ¾-inch cubes. Chill the cubed cantaloupe and the shells, which you may scallop or notch around the edges, if you wish. Whip cream, sweeten with powdered sugar, flavor with vanilla, and fold in the chilled cubed cantaloupe. Divide the mixture among the cantaloupe shells, and garnish each with 6 or 8 pitted Bing cherries. Serve in soup bowls that you have filled with finely crushed ice. Makes 6 servings.

Gingered Tropical Fruits

Arrange fruits on a tray or on individual plates; pass the sauce to add to taste. Or you can use just sliced oranges or bananas with the sauce; you'll need 6 to 8 of either fruit.

1 small fresh pineapple (or half a large
  one)
2 oranges
1 papaya
3 bananas
1 lemon
Mint leaves
Ginger Sauce (directions follow)

Peel pineapple, oranges, and papaya. Slice pineapple and oranges into thin rounds; seed papaya and cut in slices lengthwise. Peel bananas and cut in thick slices on a slant; sprinkle with lemon juice to prevent darkening.

Arrange fruit attractively on a platter and garnish with mint leaves. Serve sauce in a small bowl. Invite people to make their own servings. Makes 6 to 8 servings.

Ginger Sauce. Blend 1 cup sour cream and 1½ tablespoons *each* honey and chopped candied ginger; cover and chill.

Pineapple Hawaiian

Arrange 1 slice fresh pineapple on each plate; top with a scoop of vanilla ice cream (or lemon ice), pour a tablespoon of syrup from preserved ginger (or rum) on each portion, and sprinkle with freshly grated coconut.

Dates in Cream

Slice pitted dates into sherbet dishes. Pour over heavy cream or light cream flecked with nutmeg or grated orange peel. Serve chilled with crisp cookies or hot coffee.

Minted Pineapple

Select a ripe pineapple, peel, and cut in cubes. Arrange on scoops of lemon ice; pour 1 tablespoon crème de menthe over each portion, and garnish with mint leaves.

Upside-Down Pears

Remove stems and cut thin slices from the bottoms of ripe pears; remove cores. Enlarge opening slightly and fill with chopped glacéed fruits, or a favorite preserve, or chopped ginger. Drizzle in a little liqueur, if you wish. Put pears, stem end down, in wine glasses or any glass in which they fit snugly. Garnish tops with whipped cream, and serve with a spoon.

Pear and Cherry Compote

2 cans (1 lb. 13 oz.) each *pears*
3 cans (about 1 lb. each) *pitted sweet cherries*
1 tablespoon *vanilla*
Blanched almonds

Drain the juices from both fruits, and simmer until reduced to approximately ⅓ of the original volume. Add vanilla. Put half a blanched almond in each cherry. Arrange pears around edge of a yellow shallow bowl, put cherries in the middle. Pour the syrup over the fruit, and chill before serving. Makes about 12 servings.

Chafing Dish Apples

4 large cooking apples
½ cup Jamaican rum or dark rum
Flour
½ cup (¼ pound) butter
¼ cup powdered sugar
Commercial sour cream
Sugar

Peel, core, and slice apples, and cover with rum. Let stand for 3 hours. Drain (reserving rum); dry the apples and dust them lightly with flour. In chafing dish, melt butter; sauté apples until nicely browned on both sides. Sprinkle with powdered sugar and reserved rum, and when it is hot, ignite the rum. When flames die down, serve with cold sour cream and a shaker of sugar. Makes 5 or 6 servings.

Broiled Pineapple and Banana with Ice Cream

For a spectacular dessert, broil pineapple and banana with butter and brown sugar, and serve the caramel-glazed fruit piping hot with a topping of vanilla ice cream melting over the top.

3 ripe bananas
6 slices canned or fresh pineapple
⅓ cup firmly packed brown sugar
¼ cup butter
1 tablespoon lemon juice
1 pint vanilla ice cream

Cut each banana in half lengthwise and then crosswise to make 4 pieces—2 for each serving.

Arrange the banana pieces and pineapple slices in a single layer in a baking dish. Sprinkle brown sugar over the top, dot with butter, and sprinkle with lemon juice. Set the fruit about 8 inches below your broiler and broil, basting several times, for 5 to 7 minutes, or until the fruit is glazed. Serve hot into individual dessert dishes, top with a scoop of vanilla ice cream, then spoon some of the hot butter sauce over top of ice cream. Makes 6 servings.

Baked Pineapple Guavas

Baking brings out the tart-sweet flavor of pineapple guavas, which can be home grown in your garden on an attractive shrub.

3 pineapple guavas
½ cup sugar
⅛ teaspoon salt
2 tablespoons lemon juice
2 tablespoons butter
Sweetened whipped cream

Cut guavas in half; carefully scoop out centers, leaving shells intact. Remove seeds from centers; mix seeded pulp with sugar, salt, lemon juice. Spoon into shells and dot with butter. Place in a shallow baking dish that has 2 or 3 tablespoons water in the bottom. Cover and bake in a moderate oven (350°) for 25 minutes, or until tender. Cool. Top each serving with whipped cream. Makes 3 servings.

Cantaloupe à la Mode with Wine-Blueberry Sauce

If you are fond of cantaloupe with ice cream, you'll like this dessert.

½ cup sugar
1 tablespoon cornstarch
3 thin lemon slices
¾ cup port wine or grape juice
1½ to 2 cup blueberries (fresh or frozen)
Firm vanilla ice cream
Cantaloupe rings or halves

In a small saucepan, combine sugar, cornstarch, lemon slices, and wine or grape juice. Simmer about 5 minutes, or until clear. Remove lemon, add blueberries, and chill thoroughly. Spoon ice cream into melon rings or halves, and top with the chilled blueberry sauce. Makes about 1¾ cups sauce, enough for 6 to 8 servings.

Cherry Compote

Leave stems on cherries and poach in red wine (½ cup sugar to each cup wine) for 5 minutes. Let cool in the syrup, then remove to a bowl, arranging with stems sticking into the air. Reduce wine until thick; add 1 tablespoon currant jelly for each ½ cup syrup, melt, then add 1 or 2 drops almond extract; pour over cherries. Chill.

Flaming Dessert Bananas

2 or 3 medium ripe bananas
3 tablespoons butter
½ teaspoon grated orange peel
2 tablespoons sugar
¼ cup Cointreau or curaçao, warmed
Sweetened whipped cream

Peel bananas, cut in half lengthwise and then crosswise. Melt butter in a chafing dish over direct flame. Add orange peel and the bananas, cut side up. Cook quickly until lightly browned; turn cut sides down into butter. Sprinkle with sugar. Simmer until fruit is browned. Add Cointreau or curaçao, and flame. Serve fruit in bowls topped with spoonfuls of sweetened whipped cream, and then drizzle with sauce from bananas. Makes about 4 servings.

Crêpes and Pancakes Desserts

Although the names are the same, the elegant flavors and dramatic ways of serving dessert pancakes bear little resemblance to the hearty stacks offered at breakfast time. Yet these impressive desserts are actually quite simple to make, and in most cases the cakes themselves require fewer ingredients than do baking powder pancakes. Dessert pancakes may be the classic, thin French crêpes, or the less well-known thick and airy souffléed French crêpes; or they may be puffy, egg-rich pancakes baked in a frying pan or in the oven.

The thin French crêpes called for in many of the recipes can be made in advance and frozen until you are ready to use them. To freeze crêpes, make stacks of 6 to 12 crêpes, wrap airtight in foil, and freeze. Thaw completely before separating; allow about 3 hours at room temperature, or place the foil-wrapped crêpes in a warm oven (175°) for about 20 minutes.

French Crêpes

You cook these thin pancakes in a lightly buttered omelet pan or you may use a 10-inch frying pan to make three or four smaller crêpes at a time.

3 eggs
1 cup milk
¾ cup all-purpose flour (sift before
  measuring)
1 tablespoon sugar
¼ teaspoon salt
Butter

In a small mixing bowl, beat eggs well and mix in milk until smooth. Sift flour again with sugar and salt. Add dry ingredients to egg mixture and beat with electric mixer until batter is smooth. Set aside in a cool place for at least 1 hour.

Place omelet pan (for regular-size, 6-inch crêpes) or a 10-inch frying pan (for smaller, 3-inch crêpes) over medium heat. When pan is hot, add ½ teaspoon butter and coat pan. Slowly pour batter onto pan, spreading it into a circle. (Use 2 tablespoons batter for regular-size crêpes or 1 tablespoon batter for

Finnish oven pancakes, apricot pannukakku, call for last-minute preparations, are served warm (recipe, page 75).

smaller ones.) In about 30 seconds, or when surface appears dry, turn with a spatula and cook other side until lightly browned. Remove crêpe from pan. Repeat procedure, stacking crêpes as they are cooked, and adding ½ teaspoon butter for each batch of four. Makes 16 regular-size or about 40 small crêpes.

Crêpes Kahlua

¾ cup butter
½ cup sugar
½ cup macaroon crumbs
½ cup Kahlúa or other coffee-flavored
  liqueur
24 French crêpes (5 or 6 inches in
  diameter)
½ cup (¼ pound) butter
1 pint heavy cream, whipped
Additional Kahlúa

Make filling by creaming together the ¾ cup butter, sugar, macaroon crumbs, and Kahlúa. Spread mixture on pancakes and roll. When it's time to serve, heat crêpes in the ½ cup butter in a chafing dish or electric frying pan. Serve with whipped cream and a drizzle of Kahlúa. Makes 12 servings (2 crêpes per serving).

Skewered Crêpes with Kumquats

These tiny, tender crêpes fold over plump preserved kumquats, taco-fashion. If kumquats are large, slice them in half. For a more elaborate dessert, serve the skewered kumquats with vanilla ice cream.

24 small French crêpes, 2½ to 3 inches in
   diameter (see recipe page 73)
Melted butter
Sugar
24 preserved kumquats with syrup

Brush crêpes with melted butter, sprinkle with sugar; keep warm in oven. Drain kumquats, reserving syrup for use in sauce. Enclose whole kumquat (or half kumquat, if they are large) in each crêpe. Arrange 3 on a decorative skewer for each serving. Slip quickly under broiler just before serving with warm sauce. Makes 8 servings.

Ginger-Wine Sauce
½ cup syrup drained from kumquats
White port wine or muscatel
1 teaspoon chopped preserved ginger

Thin kumquat syrup with a little white port wine or muscatel. Heat with the chopped preserved ginger. Serve warm.

Crêpes Flambé

These folded crêpe triangles simmer in a rich sauce until it begins to caramelize. Flame with an orange-flavored liqueur.

½ cup (¼ pound) butter
⅔ cup sugar (or vanilla-flavored sugar)
½ teaspoon grated orange peel
¼ teaspoon grated lemon peel
6 to 8 French crêpes, folded into
   triangles (see recipe page 73)
⅓ cup curaçao, Cointreau,
   or Triple Sec

In a shallow chafing dish or electric frying pan, combine the butter, sugar, orange and lemon peel; place over the direct flame or turn the frying pan to 250° and cook, stirring, until the mixture bubbles. Place the folded crêpes into the bubbling sauce and cook about 5 minutes longer, turning the crêpes to coat both sides; baste occasionally with more sauce. When the sugar begins to caramelize, pour the curaçao over top; ignite. Serve on small plates with hot sauce spooned over each serving. Makes 6 to 8 servings.

Souffléed French Crêpes

You usually think of a French crêpe as a very thin, tender pancake. But a crêpe also can be puffy and omelet-like. This thick, airy crêpe has beaten egg whites folded into the batter. Use it to make the Fig Crêpe Dessert or the Orange-Honey Crêpes that follow; or serve it rolled around fresh berries and topped with whipped cream.

¾ cup all-purpose flour (sift before
   measuring)
½ teaspoon each baking powder
   and salt
6 eggs, separated
1½ cups light cream or whole milk

Sift flour again with the baking powder and salt into the large bowl of your electric mixer. In the small bowl of your mixer, beat the egg whites until they form thick, satiny peaks. Slightly beat yolks with a fork, mix in cream, and add gradually to flour mixture, beating until smooth. Fold whites into the first mixture until thoroughly blended. Fry 8-inch pancakes in a generously buttered omelet pan or large frying pan—use about ½ cup batter for each crêpe and spread it to the desired size with the back of a large spoon, making certain that it is no thicker in the middle than on the sides. Cook over medium heat until just golden on both sides. Stack until ready to use. Makes 12 to 15 crêpes.

Fig Crêpe Dessert

While figs are used in this recipe, you can also make it with strawberries; substitute curls of unsweetened chocolate for the sliced walnuts on top.

½ pint (1 cup) heavy cream, chilled
1½ tablespoons granulated sugar
1 tablespoon rum (or rum flavoring
    to taste)
5 or 6 souffléed French crêpes (see recipe, facing page)
½ cup sliced walnuts
1 can (1 lb.) Kadota figs, drained and
    halved
Powdered sugar

Whip cream until stiff, beat in the sugar and rum. Spoon about 3 tablespoons of the cream down the center of each crêpe; sprinkle 1 tablespoon nuts over each strip of cream; top with a row of about 4 fig halves. Fold up sides to overlap (secure with toothpick if necessary). Place on serving plate; sprinkle with powdered sugar and remaining nuts. Serve immediately, or chill up to two hours. Makes 5 or 6 servings.

Orange-Honey Crêpes

This stack of souffléed crêpes has an orange-honey sauce spooned between the layers. You can make it several hours in advance and reheat it in the oven just before garnishing and serving.

½ cup each mild honey and butter
1 large orange (juice and grated peel)
12 souffléed French crêpes (see recipe, facing page)
Canned mandarin orange sections,
    drained (about half an 11 oz. can)
2 tablespoons toasted, slivered almonds

In a small saucepan, combine the honey, butter, and the orange juice and grated orange peel; heat and stir to blend. Stack crêpes on a heat-proof plate; spoon 1 tablespoon of orange sauce over each layer as you go. Place the completed stack in a slow oven (300°) for 12 to 15 minutes. Garnish with drained mandarins and slivered almonds. Heat extra sauce and pass it to be spooned over individual servings. Cut in wedges to serve. Makes 8 to 10 servings.

Apricot Pannukakku

Warm apricot jam makes the filling between the three layers of this pancake dessert from Finland. It must be served warm, so you bake the oven pancakes and assemble the dessert at the last minute; but you can prepare the batter several hours in advance and refrigerate it.

1 cup all-purpose flour (sift before
    measuring)
½ cup (¼ pound) soft butter or
    margarine
1 quart milk
7 eggs, unbeaten
1½ cups apricot jam
½ pint (1 cup) heavy cream
1 tablespoon powdered sugar
¼ cup powdered sugar

In the top of a double boiler, blend flour with soft butter. Gradually stir in milk and cook over simmering water until thickened. Cool mixture to lukewarm; beat in eggs, one at a time. Pour into three greased 9-inch cake pans (pans with removable bottoms are ideal) and bake in a very hot oven (400°) for about 30 minutes, or until the layers are puffed and golden brown.

Meanwhile, heat jam in a saucepan over low heat and keep warm. Whip the cream, sweetening it with 1 tablespoon powdered sugar (you can whip cream an hour or two in advance and refrigerate until you use it).

Remove all three layers of pannukakku from the oven. Gently turn out one layer onto a heavily buttered plate, then carefully slide it onto the serving platter; spoon half of the warm jam evenly over the top. Turn out the second layer on the buttered plate; slide it onto the jam-topped first layer and spoon remaining warm jam over it. Turn out the third layer in the same manner and slide it onto second layer. Sift the ¼ cup powdered sugar evenly over the top. Serve immediately by cutting in wedges and topping each wedge with the sweetened whipped cream (or pass the whipped cream at the table). Makes 8 servings.

Blintzers with Orange Sauce

These thin crêpes are rolled around a tangy blintz-type cheese filling and topped with a hot caramel-orange sauce.

1 cup ricotta cheese, or 1 small package
  (3 oz.) cream cheese blended with ⅔
  cup cottage cheese
¼ cup sugar
1 teaspoon vanilla
½ teaspoon grated lemon peel
½ teaspoon salt
16 small French crêpes, 3 to 4 inches in
  diameter (see recipe page 73)
Melted butter
Sugar

Combine cheese, sugar, vanilla, lemon peel, and salt. Fill each crêpe with about 1 tablespoon filling. Roll and place in a lightly buttered shallow baking and serving pan. Keep warm in a moderate oven (350°). Before serving, brush with melted butter and sprinkle with sugar. Serve 2 blintzers to each person. Pass caramel-orange sauce. Makes 8 servings.

Caramel-Orange Sauce

¼ cup butter
1 tablespoon flour
¼ cup each firmly packed brown sugar,
  maple-flavored syrup, dry sherry,
  orange juice, and water
2 tablespoons lemon juice
½ teaspoon grated orange peel

Heat butter with flour until butter is bubbly. Stir in brown sugar, maple-flavored syrup, sherry, orange juice, water, lemon juice, and orange peel. Bring to a boil, then simmer until well blended, about 3 minutes. Makes about 1⅓ cups.

Caramel Pear Crêpes

Serve this chafing dish dessert steaming hot. You can flame it with brandy.

1 can (1 lb.) sliced pears in heavy syrup
⅓ cup brown sugar, firmly packed
½ teaspoon grated lemon peel
1 small package (3 oz.) cream cheese
1 tablespoon brandy (or 1 tablespoon
  milk and brandy flavoring to taste)
1 tablespoon granulated sugar
⅓ cup sliced almonds
6 French crêpes (see recipe page 73)
¼ cup brandy (optional)

Drain the syrup from the canned pears into a small saucepan; stir in the brown sugar and lemon peel, heat just until boiling and until the sugar is dissolved; reduce heat to keep warm.

Make the filling by combining in a small bowl the cream cheese, 1 tablespoon brandy, and granulated sugar; blend with a fork until smooth. Stir in almonds, reserving 1 tablespoon. Carefully spread the crêpes with the cream cheese mixture to about ¾ inch from the edge. Place about 3 pear slices on one quarter of the crêpe with the ends coming to a point in the center and pointing out to the outer edge. Fold crêpe over them, forming a triangular case. Place in a chafing dish; pour the heated sauce over top. Sprinkle with the remaining almond slices. Place over heat at the table. You can substitute an electric frying pan for the chafing dish—use medium heat.)

To flame, pour the ¼ cup brandy over crêpes in the steaming sauce and ignite. Serve immediately on small plates, spooning sauce over top. Makes 6 servings.

Dutch Babies

These popover-type pancakes puff up as they bake in the oven. Serve one to a person for dessert.

3 eggs
½ cup all-purpose flour (sift before
   measuring)
½ teaspoon salt
½ cup milk
2 tablespoons melted butter
Lemon wedges
Powdered sugar
Melted butter

Using a French whip or fork, beat eggs until blended. Sift flour again with salt. Add flour and salt to eggs in 4 additions, beating after each addition just until mixture is smooth. Add milk in 2 additions, beating slightly after each. Lightly beat in melted butter. Generously butter three 5 or 6-inch baking pans (little pie pans or frying pans). Fill each with ⅓ of the mixture. Bake in a hot oven (400°) for 20 minutes; reduce heat to 350° and bake for 10 minutes more. Slip immediately onto hot plates. Offer lemon wedges, powdered sugar, and melted butter. Makes 3 servings.

Chocolate Pancake Tower

This dessert is a show-off. Your guests will be impressed by its appearance and delighted with its taste. Slice it into wedges and serve with a dark chocolate sauce (you can use canned chocolate syrup, but add a little rum or instant coffee powder and cinnamon for flavor).

4 tablespoons butter
4 tablespoons sugar
½ cup all-purpose flour (sift before
   measuring)
¼ teaspoon salt
1½ cups milk
1 teaspoon vanilla
6 eggs, separated
3 ounces semi-sweet chocolate,
   coarsely grated
2 egg whites
½ cup sugar

In a saucepan, melt butter: blend in sugar, flour, and salt. Gradually add milk; cook and stir over medium heat until mixture thickens and is smooth. Turn into large mixing bowl; cool slightly. Add vanilla. Beat egg whites until stiff, but not dry. Beat egg yolks and add to milk mixture. Fold in beaten egg whites. Bake entire recipe into pancakes in a lightly buttered, heated pan, 6 inches in diameter. Use about ⅓ cup of the batter for each. Lightly brown the pancakes on both sides.

Stack pancakes as you bake them, sprinkling each with grated chocolate. Beat the 2 egg whites just until stiff. Whip in the ½ cup sugar gradually and beat until whites hold soft, glossy peaks. Pile this meringue on top of pancake stack and brown in a moderate oven (350°). Cut into wedges to serve. Makes 6 servings.

Eiderdown Pancakes

Named for their lighter-than-ordinary, feather-like delicacy, these make a perfect dessert when served simply with powdered sugar and lemon juice, or with a favorite preserve.

6 eggs, separated
1 cup commercial sour cream
1 tablespoon sugar
½ teaspoon salt
½ cup all-purpose flour, unsifted

Beat egg yolks until thick and light colored. Stir in sour cream. Sift together sugar, salt, and flour, and stir in. Beat egg whites until stiff but not dry, and fold into the mixture. Fry by spoonfuls in butter. Makes 6 servings.

Cookies

There are many, many recipes for cookies; but this particular group has been selected for this book because these are ideal dessert cookies or dessert accompaniments. Some are hearty, some chewy, or spicy, or fruity. And some are delicious confections that can only be described as a cross between a candy and a cooky. Serve them with after-dinner coffee or to accompany fruit, sherbet, or ice cream.

Whole Wheat Refrigerator Cookies

This crisp refrigerator cooky has a sesame seed edge and a mild coffee-orange flavor. The cooky bars can be frozen for later use. When ready to bake, partially thaw, then bake as directed.

1 cup butter or margarine
1 cup brown sugar, firmly packed
1 egg
1½ cup quick-cooking rolled oats
2¼ cups unsifted whole wheat flour
1 teaspoon instant coffee powder
1 teaspoon grated orange peel
¼ cup sesame seed

Let butter stand at room temperature until softened; cream butter and brown sugar together until fluffy. Add egg and beat well. Stir in oats, whole wheat flour, instant coffee powder, and orange peel until well blended. Divide dough in half; shape each half into a bar about 12 by 2½ by 1 inches. Roll each bar in sesame seed to coat on all sides. Wrap in waxed paper and chill in the refrigerator or freezer until firm.

When ready to bake cookies, cut bars into ¼-inch slices, place on an ungreased cooky sheet, and bake in a moderate oven (350°) for 12 to 15 minutes, or until lightly browned. Makes about 8 dozen cookies.

Almond Oat Cookies

This crisp, rich cooky has the marvelous flavor and texture of blanched almonds.

⅔ cup sugar
⅔ cup butter or margarine
3 cups quick-cooking rolled oats
1 egg, beaten
1 teaspoon almond extract
½ cup slivered blanched almonds

Cream sugar and butter together; mix in rolled oats. Add the beaten egg, almond extract, and almonds; blend well. Mold into walnut-sized balls; place on a greased baking sheet and flatten to a ¼-inch thickness with a fork. Bake in a moderately hot oven (375°) about 10 minutes. Makes 2½ dozen cookies.

Hawaiian cookies (left) and brown sugar shortbread cookies (right) are perfect for afternoon tea (recipes, pages 84, 85).

Ribbon Cakes

These gay, jelly-striped cookies are baked in an unusual way. They'll keep in a tightly covered tin for six weeks.

3 cups all-purpose flour, unsifted
1 cup sugar
1 teaspoon baking powder
1 cup (½ pound) soft butter or
*   margarine*
2 whole eggs plus 1 egg white
½ teaspoon vanilla
1 cup jelly or jam (plum, blackberry, or
*   raspberry jelly, or apricot jam)*
2 tablespoons sugar

In a large bowl, mix together flour, sugar, and baking powder. Blend in butter with hands or pastry blender until mixture is like cornmeal. Add eggs, egg white, and vanilla; work into a stiff dough. Divide into two balls, one twice the size of the other. On a heavily floured board (¼ to ½ cup flour), roll out larger ball to ⅛-inch thickness; place in a cooky pan (11 by 15½ inches), smoothing out to edges and patching corners. Spread jelly over the top. Roll out remaining dough to ⅛-inch thickness and cut in ½-inch strips; place diagonally across jelly ½ inch apart. Sprinkle 2 tablespoons sugar over top.

Start baking in a moderately hot oven (375°). The edges will be done first; when edges start to brown (about 20 minutes), take pan from oven; cut off and remove about a 3-inch strip all around the edges. Return pan to oven for 10 minutes; remove. Cut into about 1 by 2-inch rectangles. Makes 7 dozen cookies.

Chocolate Charmers

These shiny-topped cookies taste like a cross between a brownie and a meringue.

1 package (6 oz.) chocolate chips
3 egg whites
1 cup powdered sugar
½ cup soda cracker crumbs
½ cup chopped pecans or walnuts
1 teaspoon vanilla

Melt chocolate over warm (not hot) water, stirring several times as it melts; cool slightly. Beat egg whites until they form soft peaks; add sugar, 2 tablespoons at a time, and continue beating until stiff but not dry. Fold in cracker crumbs, chopped nuts, vanilla, and chocolate. Drop meringue by the teaspoonful onto a greased cooky sheet. Bake in a moderately slow oven (325°) for 12 minutes. Makes 3 dozen cookies.

Lemon Squares

Lemon Squares can be served as cookies, or the squares can be cut larger and topped with vanilla ice cream for dessert.

¾ cup all-purpose flour (sift before
*   measuring)*
⅓ cup butter
2 eggs
1 cup brown sugar, firmly packed
¾ cup flaked coconut
⅛ teaspoon baking powder
½ teaspoon vanilla
⅔ cup powdered sugar
1 tablespoon grated lemon peel
1½ tablespoons lemon juice

In a bowl, finely cut butter into flour; pat out evenly to cover bottom of a 7 by 11-inch pan. Bake in a moderate oven (350°) for 10 minutes. Meanwhile, beat eggs and mix in brown sugar, coconut, baking powder, and vanilla. Spread egg mixture over baked base. Bake an additional 20 minutes at the same temperature. Blend together powdered sugar, lemon peel, and lemon juice. Frost cookies with this mixture while they are still very hot. Cut into 2-inch squares. Makes about 1½ dozen cookies.

Peanut Blossom Cookies

A chocolate candy kiss crowns each of these crunchy bite-size cookies. Try serving these hot to your guests. Bake and top with chocolate kisses ahead of time; just before serving, reheat in a warm oven.

½ cup shortening
¼ cup peanut butter
½ cup granulated sugar
½ cup brown sugar, firmly packed
1 egg
1 teaspoon vanilla
1¾ cups all-purpose flour (sift before
    measuring)
1 teaspoon soda
½ teaspoon salt
Granulated sugar
About 2 packages (5¾ oz. each)
    chocolate candy kisses

Cream together until thoroughly blended shortening, peanut butter, ½ cup granulated sugar, and brown sugar. Add the egg and vanilla and beat well. Sift flour again with soda and salt; blend into creamed mixture. Shape scant teaspoonfuls of dough into balls; roll each in granulated sugar and set on greased baking sheet. Bake in moderate oven (350°) for 8 to 10 minutes; remove. Top each with a chocolate kiss, pressing down until cooky cracks around edge. Bake for 3 to 5 minutes more. Makes 6 dozen cookies.

No-Bake Choco-Nut Cookies

3 cups quick-cooking rolled oats
5 tablespoons cocoa
½ cup chopped nuts
½ cup shredded coconut
2 cups sugar
½ cup milk
½ cup butter or margarine

In a bowl combine the oats, cocoa, nuts, and coconut. In a pan put sugar, milk, and butter or margarine; bring just to a boil, stirring to combine. Pour over the rolled oats mixture. Mix lightly until blended. Drop from a teaspoon onto waxed paper or foil. Let stand until firm, about 10 minutes. Makes about 4 dozen cookies.

Macadamia Nut Squares

These sweet, rich cookies are best served in small portions. Cashews or walnuts can be substituted for the macadamia nuts.

1 cup all-purpose flour, unsifted
½ cup butter or margarine
2 eggs, slightly beaten
½ cup grated or flaked coconut
2 tablespoons flour
1½ cups brown sugar, firmly packed
¼ teaspoon baking powder
½ teaspoon salt
1 teaspoon vanilla
1 cup chopped macadamia nuts
2 tablespoons soft butter
1½ cups powdered sugar
3 tablespoons orange juice
1 teaspoon lemon juice
½ cup ground macadamia nuts

Mix the 1 cup flour and ½ cup butter to fine crumbs; pat into the bottom of a buttered 9-inch square baking pan. Bake in a moderate oven (350°) until delicate brown, about 15 minutes. Remove from the oven and cover with a mixture of the eggs, coconut, 2 tablespoons flour, brown sugar, baking powder, salt, vanilla, and chopped nuts. Continue baking for 20 minutes. Remove from oven and cool. When cool, spread with a mixture of the 2 tablespoons butter, powdered sugar, orange juice, and lemon juice. Sprinkle ground nuts over top. Cut in small squares. Makes about 36.

English Toffee Cookies

The flavor of these cookies resembles that of English toffee candy. They are thin, crisp squares with a generous nut topping. It is easy to make a large quantity of them for serving a crowd because you spread the dough on a cooky sheet, then cut them in squares after they're baked.

1 cup butter or margarine
1 cup sugar
1 egg, separated
2 cups all-purpose flour (sift before measuring)
1 teaspoon cinnamon
1 cup chopped pecans or walnuts

Cream the butter or margarine and sugar together until smooth. Add the egg yolk, and mix in thoroughly. Sift flour again with the cinnamon. Add flour to the creamed mixture, using your hands to blend together lightly but thoroughly. Spread in an even layer over the entire surface of a greased cooky sheet (10 by 15 inches). Work with your palms to smooth the surface. Beat the egg white slightly; spread on top to completely cover. Sprinkle the chopped nuts over all, pressing them into the dough. Bake in a very slow oven (275°) for 1 hour. Cut in 1½-inch squares while still hot. Cool. Makes 6 dozen 1½-inch squares.

Spiced Prune Cookies

These are moist and chewy oatmeal cookies, full of prunes and chocolate. If you don't have prunes already cooked, use the very soft dried prunes you can buy, and you won't need to cook them.

½ cup shortening
1 cup brown sugar, firmly packed
½ cup granulated sugar
1 egg
½ cup light corn syrup
2¼ cups all-purpose flour (sift before measuring)
2 teaspoons baking powder
¾ teaspoon soda
1 teaspoon salt
1½ teaspoons each powdered ginger and cinnamon
2 cups pitted chopped cooked prunes
1 cup chopped walnuts
1 package (6 oz.) chocolate chips
1 cup quick-cooking rolled oats

Cream together shortening and both sugars. Add egg and syrup, and beat the mixture well. Sift flour again with baking powder, soda, salt, ginger, and cinnamon into creamed mixture. Beat until well blended. Stir in prunes, nuts, chocolate chips, and rolled oats. Drop by teaspoonfuls on a greased cooky sheet. Bake in a hot oven (400°) about 10 minutes. Cool on racks, then store in a tightly covered cooky jar (they'll keep well for several weeks). Makes 7 to 8 dozen cookies.

Mincemeat Bars

¼ cup butter or margarine
1 cup light brown sugar, firmly packed
1 egg
½ teaspoon vanilla
½ cup prepared mincemeat
1 cup all-purpose flour (sift before measuring)
1 teaspoon baking powder
¼ teaspoon salt

Melt butter, blend in sugar. Beat in egg, vanilla, and mincemeat. Sift flour again with the baking powder and salt; blend well with first mixture. Spread dough in a greased 8-inch square pan. Bake in a moderate oven (350°) for 35 minutes. Cool. Cut into 2-inch squares and coat with powdered sugar; or cut into larger squares and top with ice cream. Makes 16 cookies.

Basler Läckerli

In the Swiss city of Basel, *backereien* (bakeries) produce these cookies in various sizes and shapes. The small cutout cookies may be left plain, or sandwiched with filling, frosted, and adorned with nuts, colored sugar, or candied fruits.

1 cup honey
¾ cup light brown sugar, firmly packed
¼ cup butter or margarine
1 teaspoon cinnamon
½ teaspoon cloves
½ teaspoon nutmeg
1 egg, beaten
3 cups all-purpose flour (sift before
   measuring)
¼ teaspoon salt
¼ teaspoon soda
¼ cup chopped candied orange peel
¼ cup chopped candied lemon peel
2 tablespoons Kirsch or orange juice
¾ cup finely ground filberts

Place honey, sugar, butter, cinnamon, cloves, and nutmeg in a saucepan, and heat until sugar is dissolved and butter melts; turn into a bowl and let cool to lukewarm. Mix in the beaten egg. Sift flour again with salt and soda; mix into the batter. Let candied fruit peels marinate in the Kirsch or orange juice a few minutes, and mix into the batter along with nut meats. Chill dough at least 1 hour.

Then roll out a small piece at a time on a lightly floured board to about ⅜ inch thick, and cut out holiday designs with small cooky cutters. Place on lightly greased baking sheets and bake in a hot oven (400°) for 6 to 8 minutes, or until browned. Remove and cool on rack.

Store in a tightly covered container. This cooky is best aged a week before it is eaten, and it will keep three weeks at room temperature, tightly covered. Makes about 8 dozen single cookies.

Nürnberger Lebkuchen

A time-honored Christmas specialty of central Europe, these spicy honey cookies are frosted like rich confections. For mass production at home, bake in three large, thin sheets, then cut into strips and squares.

5 eggs
¾ cup light brown sugar, firmly
   packed
½ cup honey
1 tablespoon cinnamon
½ teaspoon nutmeg
½ teaspoon cloves
½ teaspoon cardamom
1 teaspoon grated lemon peel
½ pound finely ground filberts
½ pound finely ground
   unblanched almonds
½ cup chopped candied citron
½ cup orange peel

Beat eggs until light and lemon-colored, and gradually add the sugar, beating until thick. Beat in the honey and spices. Fold in lemon peel, ground nuts, and chopped fruit, mixing well. Grease a 10 by 15-inch baking sheet and line with waxed paper; grease and flour the paper.

Pour in a third of the cooky batter and spread evenly with a spatula. Bake in a moderately slow oven (300°) for 30 minutes, or until golden brown and set. Remove from oven and immediately turn out upside down on a large cake rack. Peel off the paper and let cool.

Repeat, baking two more cooky sheets with remaining batter.

When cooky sheets are cold, place on a cutting board and with a sharp knife cut into 2-inch-wide strips across the narrow side. Then cut across into 2-inch squares. If you wish, sift powdered sugar over the tops. Store in a container with a tight-fitting lid, with waxed paper between layers. Cookies can be eaten at once, or will keep up to three weeks at room temperature, tightly covered. Makes about 10 dozen.

Cialde

Traditionally made for the holiday seasons in Italy, these thin, rolled, anise cookies are baked, one at a time, in a special patterned iron, then rolled immediately. In this country, smaller and lighter Scandinavian wafer irons or flat Italian pizzelle irons make ideal substitutes for the heavier Italian cialde iron, and most people prefer their ease of handling. These irons are available in household specialty shops, in houseware sections of many department stores, and even in some delicatessens.

2 cups sugar
2 eggs
1 tablespoon vanilla
4 tablespoons each salad oil and anise-flavored liqueur or whiskey
1⅓ cups water
1 tablespoon whole anise seeds
3 cups all-purpose flour, unsifted

Beat sugar and eggs together thoroughly. Blend in vanilla, salad oil, liqueur, water, and anise seeds. Stir flour into batter. Pour one or two spoonfuls of batter in center of hot cialde (or wafer cooky) iron. (Iron is hot enough when a drop of water dances when sprinkled on top.) Clamp iron shut; scrape off overflow (you'll soon learn to judge amount.)

Bake over medium-high heat on a gas or electric burner for 1 to 2 minutes, turning frequently. Open iron just a little to see if done; when cooky is light brown, remove from heat. Ease cooky free with spatula; quickly roll to form a cylinder. Return iron to heat immediately—it must be kept hot. Scrape off any bits of cooky that stick to iron. If batter thickens, thin to original consistency with more milk. Store cookies in airtight container. Makes about 2½ dozen cookies 7 inches in diameter, or 5 dozen cookies 5 inches in diameter.

Brown Sugar Shortbreads

1 cup (½ lb.) butter or margarine, softened
1¼ cups dark brown sugar, firmly packed
1 teaspoon vanilla
2½ cups all-purpose flour (sift before measuring)

Cream butter and gradually mix in brown sugar, creaming well. Add vanilla and flour, beating until smooth. Pat into a ball, wrap in clear plastic film, and refrigerate for 1 hour. Roll out on a lightly floured board about ¼-inch thick, then cut out shapes with cutters. Place on a greased baking sheet and bake in a slow oven (300°) for 20 minutes. Makes about 3½ dozen cookies.

Sesame Seed Cookies

These wafer-thin cookies are very crisp and have a rich flavor of buttered and toasted sesame seeds.

1 teaspoon butter or margarine
½ cup sesame seed
¾ cup butter or margarine
1½ cups brown sugar, firmly packed
2 eggs
1½ cups all-purpose flour (sift before measuring)
½ teaspoon baking powder
¼ teaspoon salt
1 teaspoon vanilla

Melt the 1 teaspoon butter in a heavy frying pan over low heat. Add the sesame seed and stir until all are golden brown; set aside. Cream together the ¾ cup butter and brown sugar until smooth; beat in eggs. Sift flour again with baking powder and salt into the creamed mixture; mix until well blended. Stir in the vanilla and the toasted sesame seeds.

Drop the cooky dough by teaspoonfuls onto cooky sheets that have been greased and floured. Bake in a moderately slow oven (325°) for about 15 minutes, or until lightly browned. Remove cookies from pan immediately, and cool thoroughly before storing. To store, keep in a tightly covered container. Makes about 5 dozen cookies.

Frosted Coffee Cream Bars

Cake-like, these can be served in cooky-size or dessert-size squares.

½ cup shortening
1 cup brown sugar, firmly packed
1 egg
½ cup hot coffee
1⅔ cups all-purpose flour (sift before
     measuring)
½ teaspoon each baking powder, soda,
     cinnamon, and salt
½ cup seedless raisins
¼ cup chopped walnuts

Icing

1½ cups sifted powdered sugar
1 tablespoon soft butter or margarine
1 teaspoon vanilla
About 3 tablespoons hot coffee

Cream shortening with sugar; blend in egg, then coffee. Sift flour again with the baking powder, soda, cinnamon, and salt; mix well with first mixture. Stir in the raisins and walnuts. Spread batter in a greased cooky pan (11 by 16 inches) and bake in a moderately hot oven (375°) for about 15 minutes. Cool in pan, then spread with thin icing made by blending the powdered sugar, butter, vanilla, and coffee (add more coffee if needed). When icing is set, cut into squares. Makes 20 cookies about 2 inches square, or 12 servings about 3 inches square.

Hawaiian Shortbread Cookies

1 cup (½ lb.) butter or margarine
¼ cup granulated sugar
1 teaspoon vanilla
2 cups regular all-purpose flour
¼ teaspoon salt
2 cups flaked coconut
1 cup powdered sugar

Cream butter, add the granulated sugar, and cream until smooth. Mix in vanilla. Sift flour, measure, then sift again with salt; gradually add to the creamed mixture, beating until smooth. Mix in the coconut. Shape into a 1½-inch-thick roll and wrap in clear plastic film. Refrigerate.

Slice ¼ inch thick and place on a greased baking sheet. Bake in a slow oven (300°) for 20 minutes. Sift powdered sugar onto waxed paper and transfer cookies onto it. Sift additional sugar lightly on top. Let cool. Makes about 3½ dozen.

Crisp Nutmeg Cookies

Use your favorite cooky cutters for this dough flavored with nutmeg. Before rolling, the dough must be chilled thoroughly. The cookies will be thin and crisp.

1 cup soft butter
1 cup sugar
1 egg
3½ cups all-purpose flour (sift before
     measuring)
⅛ teaspoon salt
1 teaspoon ground nutmeg
1 teaspoon soda
½ cup buttermilk

Cream the butter until light and fluffy. Gradually beat in the sugar and egg. Sift flour again with the salt, nutmeg, and soda. Add to the creamed mixture alternately with the buttermilk. Shape the dough into a ball and chill several hours until firm. Roll out a small portion of dough at a time on a well floured board until very thin (keep rest of the dough in refrigerator). Cut with cooky cutters. Bake on an ungreased baking sheet in a moderate oven (350°) for 10 minutes or until lightly browned. Makes about 6 dozen cookies.

Bowknot Cookies

Tender, buttery, and delicate, these are cookies to serve with coffee at any time of day.

4 hard-cooked egg yolks
4 uncooked egg yolks
1 cup butter
1 cup sugar
3 cups all-purpose flour (sift before
   measuring)
1 egg white
Sugar

Put hard-cooked egg yolks through a ricer, or mash thoroughly. Mix with uncooked egg yolks. Cream butter and sugar well, then blend in mixed egg yolks. Blend flour with the creamed mixture. Roll dough ¼ inch thick. Use a knife to cut in strips 1 inch wide. Roll strips into a rope. Cut into 1½-inch lengths and pinch in middle to form bows. Brush with beaten white of egg, and sprinkle with sugar. Bake in a moderate oven (350°) for 8 minutes or until cookies begin to brown. Makes about 4 dozen cookies.

Wild Blackberry Cheese Squares

1¾ cups all-purpose flour (sift before
   measuring)
1 teaspoon baking powder
¼ teaspoon salt
1 tablespoon brown sugar
½ cup butter or margarine
1 cup (¼ pound) shredded mild
   Cheddar cheese
1 jar (10 oz.) wild blackberry jam

Sift flour again with baking powder, salt, and brown sugar. Cut butter and cheese into the dry ingredients until mixture is crumbly. Set aside ¾ cup of the cheese crumbs, and pat the remaining mixture into an 8-inch square baking pan. Spread jam evenly over the cheese mixture in the pan and sprinkle with the remaining cheese crumbs. Bake in a moderate oven (350°) for 25 minutes. Cool and cut into squares. Makes 16 squares.

Apple Chunkies

1 cup all-purpose flour (sift before
   measuring)
1 teaspoon baking powder
¼ teaspoon salt
¼ cup butter
¾ cup sugar
1 egg
1 teaspoon vanilla
½ cup chopped raw apple
½ cup coarsely broken walnuts

Sift flour again with baking powder and salt. Melt butter in a saucepan; remove from heat and stir in sugar. Cool slightly then beat in the egg thoroughly; add vanilla. Fold in flour mixture. Stir in apples and nuts. Spread batter into a greased 8 by 8-inch baking pan. Bake in a moderate oven (350°) for 30 minutes, until golden brown. While still warm, cut into 2-inch squares. Makes 16 cookies.

Ginger Thins

Keep these paper-thin and very crisp cookies on hand to serve with tea, ice cream, or fruit. For a delicious and more unusual dessert, serve them with seedless grapes mixed with sour cream, a little brown sugar, and a judicious amount of Jamaica rum.

½ cup dark molasses
¼ cup butter
1¾ cups all-purpose flour (sift before
   measuring)
¼ teaspoon soda
1½ teaspoons ground ginger
½ teaspoon salt

Heat together molasses and butter. Add flour, soda, ground ginger, and salt; mix well and chill thoroughly. Remove a small portion from the refrigerator at a time (it will be a little sticky and hard to work) and quickly roll paper-thin on a floured board. Cut in 2-inch circles, put on a greased cooky sheet, and bake in a moderate oven (350°) for 6 to 8 minutes, or until they just begin to brown. They should be very crisp. If properly rolled, this amount will make about 115 cookies.

Coconut-Frosted Date Balls

These cookies don't require any baking. They keep well when stored in a tightly covered container.

2 eggs
1 cup sugar
¼ teaspoon salt
1½ cups pitted dates, cut fine
2¼ cups toasted rice cereal
½ cup chopped walnuts
1 teaspoon vanilla
2 cups flaked coconut

Beat eggs with sugar and salt until thick. Add dates. Turn mixture into heavy frying pan and cook over low heat about 10 minutes, stirring. Remove from heat; add cereal, chopped walnuts, and vanilla. When mixture is cool enough to handle, pinch off portions and (with dampened hands) form into balls about the size of walnuts. Roll in flaked coconut. Makes about 48 cookies.

Lemon Pecan Refrigerator Cookies

You don't taste the lemon when you first bite into these crisp nut cookies, but you notice its flavor a moment later.

½ cup butter or margarine
1 cup sugar
1 egg
1 tablespoon grated lemon peel
1 tablespoon lemon juice
2 cups all-purpose flour (sift before
   measuring)
⅛ teaspoon salt
1 teaspoon baking powder
1 cup chopped pecans

Cream butter and sugar thoroughly. Add egg and lemon peel and juice, and beat until smooth. Sift flour again with salt and baking powder. Add dry ingredients to the creamed mixture and mix until blended. Stir in chopped pecans. Shape into 2 rolls 1½ inches in diameter, and roll up in waxed paper. Chill. Slice thinly and place on a greased baking sheet. Bake in a moderate oven (350°) for 12 minutes. Makes 6 dozen cookies.

Lackerli

The name for these spicy, cake-like cookies means "a tasty or sweet tidbit."

2 cups milk
1 cup butter or margarine
1 cup sugar
⅔ cup molasses
4 cups all-purpose flour (sift before
   measuring)
1 teaspoon salt
2 teaspoons cinnamon
½ teaspoon each ginger, cloves,
   and nutmeg
1½ teaspoons soda
2 tablespoons cocoa

Powdered Sugar Icing

2 cups sifted powdered sugar
½ teaspoon vanilla
¼ to ⅓ cup milk

Scald the 2 cups milk. Add butter, sugar, and molasses; turn into a large bowl to cool. Sift flour again with salt, spices, soda, and cocoa. Gradually add to the milk-molasses mixture, beating well after each addition. Divide the batter between two buttered large shallow baking pans (about 12 by 17 inches). Spread to the edges of the pan; batter should be between ¼ and ½ inch thick. Bake in a moderately hot oven (375°) about 15 minutes. Blend icing ingredients and spread on cookies while they are still warm. Cool. Cut diagonally into diamonds. Makes about 5 dozen cookies.

Favorite Fruit Bars

Rich and crumbly, these sweet-tart fruit bars are easiest to eat with a fork.

Filling

1 cup each *currants and raisins*
1 cup sugar
¼ teaspoon salt
1 teaspoon cinnamon
½ teaspoon cloves
1 teaspoon vinegar
4 tablespoons all-purpose flour, unsifted
1 tablespoon butter
1½ cups hot water

In a saucepan combine all filling ingredients. Bring to a boil and cook until thick, stirring constantly. Cool to room temperature.

Crust

1½ cups all-purpose flour (sift before measuring)
1 cup brown sugar, firmly packed
¼ teaspoon salt
1 teaspoon baking powder
¾ cup butter

Mix flour, brown sugar, salt, and baking powder. Cut in butter to form a crumbly mixture. Pat ⅔ of mixture into bottom of a greased baking pan (9 by 13 inches). Spread with fruit filling. Sprinkle remaining crumbs over the top. Bake in a moderate oven (350°) for 40 minutes. Cool and cut into 1 by 3-inch bars. Makes 2½ dozen cookies.

Sandkakor

These rich Swedish cookies are delicately flavored with ground cardamom.

1 cup soft butter
⅔ cup sugar
2 cups all-purpose flour (sift before measuring)
½ teaspoon ground cardamom
¼ teaspoon soda

Cream the butter until light and fluffy. Gradually beat in the sugar. Sift flour again with the ground cardamom and soda. Beat into the creamed mixture. Shape the dough into small balls, about the size of small walnuts. Place on an ungreased baking sheet; bake in a moderate oven (350°) for 10 minutes, or until golden. Makes about 8 dozen cookies.

Oversized, All-day Cookies

Giant, 5-inch-wide cookies are filled with good things —rolled oats, whole wheat, nuts, and chocolate chips. A variation substitutes raisins for the chocolate chips.

1 cup butter or margarine
1½ cups firmly packed brown sugar
2 eggs
1 teaspoon vanilla
1½ cups whole wheat or all-purpose flour, unsifted
2⅓ cups rolled oats, regular or quick-cooking
2 teaspoons soda
1 teaspoon salt
1 package (12 oz.) semisweet chocolate or butterscotch pieces
1½ cups chopped nuts

Beat butter and brown sugar together until creamy. Stir in eggs and vanilla. Add flour, oats, soda, and salt; mix until well blended. Stir in chocolate pieces and nuts.

To shape cookies, spoon dough into a ½-cup measure, level off, and turn out onto a greased cookie sheet (two cookies will fit on a 12 by 15-inch pan, three on a 14 by 17-inch pan). Space cookies at least 6 inches apart and 2½ inches from pan edge. Lightly grease the bottom of a pie pan, dip into sugar, and use to flatten each cookie into a 5-inch circle. If necessary, even out the thickness with your fingers.

Bake in a 350° oven about 15 minutes or until edges brown lightly. To bake two pans at the same time, place them in the top and bottom thirds of the oven, staggering the pans slightly. In smaller ovens you may need to switch pan positions halfway through baking to ensure even browning. Allow cookies to cool on pans about 5 minutes; transfer to racks to cool thoroughly. Makes 10 or 11 cookies.

Big Oatmeal Raisin Cookies. Follow recipe above except add 1 teaspoon ground cinnamon and ½ teaspoon ground nutmeg with flour. Omit chocolate pieces and add 1½ cups raisins.

Coconut Meringue Drops

These chewy, light, and airy meringues make delicate party cookies, ideal accompaniments for any frozen mousse or ice cream dessert. They freeze beautifully if packaged in moisture-proof rigid containers.

5 tablespoons granulated sugar
5 tablespoons powdered sugar
1 tablespoon flour
2 egg whites
¼ teaspoon vanilla
1 cup shredded coconut

Sift together the sugars and flour. Beat egg whites until foamy; gradually add dry ingredients, 2 tablespoons at a time. Beat until stiff. Fold in vanilla and coconut. Drop from a teaspoon onto an ungreased paper-lined cooky sheet. Bake in a moderately slow oven (350°) for 20 minutes, or until golden brown. Makes 8 dozen cookies.

Husarenkrapferl

These "hussars' tartlets" are rich little Viennese cookies that make a just-right nibble of sweetness to end a meal.

2 cups sifted flour
3 egg yolks
⅔ cup butter
1 cup sugar
¼ teaspoon salt
1 egg white, slightly beaten
Finely chopped almonds
Apricot jam
Powdered sugar

Combine flour, egg yolks, butter, sugar, and salt. Knead until smooth, then chill for about half an hour. Form into smooth walnut-size balls and arrange on a greased cooky sheet. Brush with slightly beaten egg white and sprinkle with almonds; with the handle of a wooden spoon or a dowel, press a deep hole in the center of each cooky. Chill again for 30 minutes, then bake in a moderate oven (350°) for 20 minutes, or until lightly browned. Remove from pan and fill the holes with apricot jam. Dust with powdered sugar and serve in little paper bon-bon cases. Makes about 3 dozen cookies.

Orange Marmalade Cookies

1 cup butter
1 cup sugar
2 eggs, beaten
¼ cup milk
1 teaspoon vanilla
2 cups all-purpose flour (sift before measuring)
⅔ teaspoon soda
½ teaspoon salt
2½ cups quick-cooking rolled oats
½ cup chopped raisins
½ cup chopped walnuts
⅔ cup orange marmalade

Cream butter and sugar. Blend in the eggs, milk, and vanilla. Sift flour again with soda and salt, and stir into first mixture. Mix in rolled oats, raisins, nuts, and marmalade. Drop from teaspoon onto lightly greased cooky sheets about 3 inches apart. Bake in a moderate oven (350°) for about 12 minutes. Makes 5 dozen cookies.

Spiced Almond Wafers

Here is a crisp, buttery refrigerator cooky that's ideal to serve with dessert or for tea time. You can refrigerate unbaked dough for about two weeks.

1 cup butter or margarine
1 cup brown sugar, firmly packed
2 cups all-purpose flour (sift before measuring)
2 teaspoons ground cinnamon
½ teaspoon ground nutmeg
¼ teaspoon soda
¼ cup commercial sour cream
½ cup slivered blanched almonds

Cream butter and sugar until light. Sift flour again with cinnamon and nutmeg. Blend soda into sour cream. Add dry ingredients alternately with sour cream, mixing until smooth. Stir in slivered almonds. Shape into rolls about 2½ inches in diameter and 6 inches long. Wrap in waxed paper and chill overnight. Slice ⅛ inch thick and place on an ungreased baking sheet. Bake in a moderate oven (350°) for 10 minutes, or until golden brown. Makes 6 dozen.

Sauces and Toppings

Almost any dessert, particularly the simpler ones like ice cream, uniced cake, or fruit, gains quick glamour when a judiciously selected sauce or topping is added as a finishing touch. Whether you need one that is thick or thin, hot or cold, smooth or crunchy, sweet or tart, you'll find an appropriate choice among these easy-to-make sauces and toppings. Some suggested ways to serve them are given with the recipes.

Fluffy Custard Sauce

Whipped cream folded into this faintly citrus-flavored custard gives the sauce a pleasant fluffiness. Try serving it with plain baked custards, or over fruits. You can make the sauce the day before; add the wine and whipped cream before serving.

1 cup light cream
⅛ teaspoon grated orange or lemon
   peel
3 egg yolks
3 tablespoons sugar
Dash salt
¼ cup dry sherry or orange juice
½ cup heavy cream, whipped
Sliced oranges
Toasted coconut

Scald cream with orange peel. Stir into egg yolks beaten with sugar and salt. Stir and cook slowly over hot (not boiling) water, until mixture clings to spoon in an even coating. Cool. Stir in wine. Fold whipped cream into sauce and pour over orange slices, sprinkle with coconut and serve. Makes about 2½ cups sauce.

Chestnut Cream Topping

Spoon this whipped cream sauce over steamed puddings, or over angel food or sponge cakes, canned fruit, or cooked prunes.

2 cups cooked, peeled chestnuts
2 tablespoons light corn syrup
⅛ teaspoon salt
¼ cup sugar
1½ teaspoons vanilla
½ pint (1 cup) heavy cream
1 teaspoon grated orange peel

Put cooked chestnuts through a fine sieve twice. Add syrup, salt, sugar, and vanilla, and beat until well blended. Whip cream and orange peel until cream is stiff and fold into the chestnut mixture. Makes about 3½ cups of topping.

raline lace crust, a quick and delicious
ay to dress up simple desserts, can be
repared in minutes (recipe, page 92).

Glazed Cranberry Sauce

Fresh cranberries are cooked into a spicy sauce to serve over vanilla ice cream.

1 cup sugar
1 stick cinnamon
2 thin slices lemon
½ cup port wine
1¾ cups fresh cranberries

Combine sugar, cinnamon, lemon, and wine. Bring to a boil; lower heat and simmer 4 or 5 minutes. Add cranberries and cook gently just until they begin to pop. Remove from heat; cool. Serve cold or reheat and serve warm. Makes 1⅔ cups.

Raspberry Sauce

Serve this whipped fruit sauce over hot steamed puddings, pound or sponge cake, or dessert waffles.

1 cup butter or margarine
2 cups sugar
2 eggs
1 package (12 oz.) frozen raspberries

Cream butter until very fluffy; gradually add sugar, beating until mixture is very light. Add eggs, one at a time, beating well after each addition. When the mixture resembles whipped cream, add raspberries, thawed to room temperature, a few at a time. Chill until ready to use. Makes about 3 cups sauce.

Sour Cream Sauce

One of the simplest of sauces to serve with fruit desserts is made by combining 1 cup sour cream with ¼ to ½ cup honey. This may be further embellished with grated coconut, crystallized ginger, or chopped nuts. It is good on all berries, peaches, pears, and seedless grapes.

Cream Cheese and Orange Sauce

1 large package (8 oz.) cream cheese
2 to 3 tablespoons honey
Grated peel of 1 orange

Whip cream cheese with the honey and orange peel. Chill. Makes 1½ cups sauce.

Praline Lace Crust

If you enjoy the flavor of caramel and the crunch of pralines, you will find many uses for this lacy brown sugar crust. It provides a quick and delectable way to dress up simple dishes. You can make it in five minutes or less, just by broiling a thin layer of brown sugar, then store until you're ready to use it. Try it as a topping for custards, ice cream or sherbet, applesauce, or tapioca or rice pudding.

Heavily butter a chilled cooky sheet (one without side rims). Sprinkle with an even layer—⅛ to ¼ inch deep—of brown sugar rubbed through a wire strainer. Leave a border of at least 1 inch on all sides.

Place 6 inches beneath heat in broiler. Watch very carefully, turning pan if necessary to cook evenly. When sugar is bubbling (this may take less than 1 minute so be careful not to scorch it), remove from heat and let cool until you can just touch pan comfortably. Then quickly and gently loosen crust with a long, flexible spatula. Store crust flat, wrapped airtight in foil or clear plastic wrap; or break in small pieces and store in a jar. Crust will stay crisp for about a week if in foil, or indefinitely if in a jar.

Chocolate Rum Sauce

Serve this easy-to-make sauce warm, over ice cream.

*1 package (6 oz.) semi-sweet chocolate
    chips*
⅔ cup heavy cream
½ cup rum

Put chocolate chips in the top of a double boiler. When the water boils, turn off heat and let stand until chocolate is almost melted, then stir until smooth. Add cream and rum; stir to combine.

Crème de Cacao Sauce

Dress up ice cream with a sauce flavored with chocolate and coffee, sharply accented with crème de cacao. This is particularly good over peppermint ice cream.

½ cup strong coffee
¼ cup sugar
¼ cup sweet ground chocolate
¼ cup crème de cacao

Combine coffee with sugar and chocolate and boil slowly for 5 minutes. Cool to room temperature. Add crème de cacao. Makes about 1 cup.

Flaming Mincemeat Sauce

Cranberry juice gives deep red color and tangy flavor to this flaming mincemeat. It's best on vanilla or eggnog ice cream.

2 cups mincemeat
1 cup cranberry juice cocktail
½ cup rum or brandy

Stir the mincemeat and cranberry juice together in a saucepan. Heat until simmering. Heat the rum or brandy in a separate small container over low heat or over hot water. Spoon a little of the hot rum onto mincemeat; ignite. Continue to pour on rum slowly, spooning mincemeat until flames die down. Makes 3 cups.

Date Pecan Sauce

Rum tones down the richness of dates in this umber-colored sauce. Serve it over vanilla ice cream or French pancakes.

1 cup coarsely chopped dates
½ cup rum
½ cup sugar
½ cup water
⅓ cup coarsely chopped pecans

Marinate dates in the rum in a covered container for 48 hours. Combine sugar and water in a saucepan and boil for 10 minutes; cool. Stir cooled syrup into the dates and rum. Just before serving, stir in the pecans. Makes 2 cups.

Cinnamon-Blueberry Sauce

Cinnamon is a very good spice with blueberries. Serve this delicious easy-to-make sauce over ice cream, plain cake, or chilled custards.

1 cup blueberries
2 tablespoons water
¼ cup sugar
¼ teaspoon cinnamon
1 teaspoon lemon juice

Combine blueberries with water, sugar, cinnamon, and lemon juice. Cook 5 minutes. Chill. Makes enough sauce to spoon over 4 to 6 servings of ice cream or cake.

Special Fruit Sauce

Serve this with strawberries, peaches, mixed fruits, or figs.

2 egg yolks
2 tablespoons sugar
1 cup milk, scalded
1 teaspoon vanilla, or 2 tablespoons
   any liqueur
2 cups heavy cream, whipped

Beat egg yolks with sugar. Pour over scalded milk, and cook in a double boiler, stirring, until the mixture coats a spoon. Cool. Flavor with the vanilla or liqueur and chill. Before serving, combine with the whipped cream.

Honey-Chocolate Sundae Sauce

Unlike some chocolate sauces that harden as soon as they are poured over cold ice cream, this honey-flavored sauce stays creamy and smooth.

½ cup butter or margarine
2 tablespoons cornstarch
½ cup cocoa
1 cup honey
1 cup water
½ teaspoon salt
12 marshmallows

Melt butter; remove from heat, and stir in cornstarch, mixed with the cocoa, until blended. Pour in honey and water. Heat, stirring constantly, until sauce comes to a boil and thickens. Remove from heat, add salt and marshmallows, and stir until marshmallows are melted. Makes 2½ cups sauce.

Crunch Cream

Fold ½ cup crushed hard candy (peppermint canes, peanut brittle, or English toffee) into 1 cup heavy cream, whipped. Serve as topping for brownies or devil's food cake. Makes about 2½ cups topping.

Brandy Plum Pudding Sauce

Especially delicious with plum pudding, this sauce is rich and creamy, yet simple and somehow light in effect. The brandy flavor is quite subtle.

1 cup sugar
½ cup butter
4 egg yolks, well beaten
1 cup whipped cream
2 to 3 tablespoons brandy

Cream together the sugar and butter. Add egg yolks and cream and beat well. Place in a double boiler and cook, stirring, until the consistency of heavy cream, but do not overcook. Add brandy and pour sauce over pudding. Serve warm or cold. Makes about 2½ cups sauce.

Index

A Handy Metric Conversion Table

To change	To	Multiply By
ounces (oz.)	grams (g)	28
pounds (lbs.)	kilograms (kg)	0.45
teaspoons	milliliters (ml)	5
tablespoons	milliliters (ml)	15
fluid ounces (oz.)	milliliters (ml)	30
cups	liters (l)	0.24
pints (pt.)	liters (l)	0.47
quarts (qt.)	liters (l)	0.95
gallons (gal.)	liters (l)	3.8
Fahrenheit temperature (°F)	*Celsius temperature (°C)*	*5/9 after subtracting 32*